SEE IT, THINK IT, SAY IT, WRITE IT, BELIEVE IT, BE IT

God Has A Plan For Your Life

Rev. Thelma C. Smith

Copyright © 2019 by Rev. Thelma C. Smith

All rights reserved. No part of this publication may be reproduced by any means, graphics, electronic, or mechanical, including photocopying, recording, taping, or by any information storage retrieval system without the written permission of the publisher except in the case of brief quotations embodied in critical articles and reviews.

Rev. Thelma C. Smith/Rejoice Essential Publishing
PO BOX 512
Effingham, SC 29541

www.republishing.org

Unless otherwise indicated, scripture is taken from the New King James Version.

Scripture quotations marked (NKJV) are taken from the New King James Version®. Copyright © 1982 by Thomas Nelson. Used by permission. All rights reserved.

Scripture quotations marked (NLT) are taken from the Holy Bible, New Living Translation, copyright ©1996, 2004, 2015 by Tyndale House Foundation. Used by permission of Tyndale House Publishers, Inc., Carol Stream, Illinois 60188. All rights reserved.

Scripture quotations marked (AMP) are taken from the Amplified Bible, Copyright © 1954, 1958, 1962, 1964, 1965, 1987 by The Lockman Foundation. Used by permission.

Scripture quotations marked AMPC are taken from the Amplified® Bible (AMPC), Copyright © 1954, 1958, 1962, 1964, 1965, 1987 by The Lockman Foundation Used by permission. www.Lockman.org"

Scripture quotations marked (NIV) are taken from the Holy Bible, New International Version®, NIV®. Copyright © 1973, 1978, 1984, 2011 by Biblica, Inc.™ Used by permission of Zondervan. All rights reserved worldwide. www.zondervan.com The "NIV" and "New International Version" are trademarks registered in the United States Patent and Trademark Office by Biblica, Inc.™

Quotations designated (NET) are from the NET Bible® copyright ©1996-2018 by Biblical Studies Press, L.L.C. http://netbible.com All rights reserved.

Scripture quotations marked (TLB) are taken from The Living Bible copyright © 1971. Used by permission of Tyndale House Publishers, a Division of Tyndale House Ministries, Carol Stream, Illinois 60188. All rights reserved.

Scripture quotations taken from the New American Standard Bible® (NASB), Copyright © 1960, 1962, 1963, 1968, 1971, 1972, 1973, 1975, 1977, 1995 by The Lockman Foundation Used by permission. www.Lockman.org"

Author's website: www.abundantglory.org

See It, Think It, Say It, Write It, Believe It, Be It/ Rev. Thelma C. Smith

ISBN-10: 1-946756-77-6

ISBN-13: 978-1-946756-77-0

Library of Congress Number: 2019916277

TABLE OF CONTENTS

INTRODUCTION:	A Time of Promotion...............1
CHAPTER ONE:	See It.....................17
CHAPTER TWO:	Think It.................28
CHAPTER THREE:	Say It....................48
CHAPTER FOUR:	Write It..................66
CHAPTER FIVE:	Believe It..............78
CHAPTER SIX:	Be It.....................96

DEDICATION

I would like to dedicate my book to one who has taught me the Word of God and blessed and helped me to grow spiritually through the years, to my wonderful husband and Pastor, Pierce Smith.

INTRODUCTION

A TIME OF PROMOTION

Ezekiel 3:14-15 (NKJV)
"So the Spirit lifted me up and took me away, and I went in bitterness, in the heat of my spirit; but the hand of the Lord was strong upon me. [15] Then I came to the captives at Tel Abib, who dwelt by the River Chebar; and I sat where they sat, and remained there astonished among them seven days."

According to the Strong's Concordance, Hebrew 3528: Chebar[1], means a great while, long ago, already, (seeing that which), or now.

You have gone to school and taken courses. You have spent time in the Word and time with God. You have fasted and prayed. You have assisted others in their work. You have begun to develop materials to support your work. You have been tested as you have walked through the fire and the flood. Now is the time. God is telling you to step up into what He has called you to do. He has called you to take possession of all that He has given you. Just as Joshua and Caleb led the tribe of Israel into the Promised Land, now is the time for you to take possession of the thing that God has promised you. There is something very special about a land grant given by God.

Now you are ready to deal with the demons, the naysayers, the giants, those who would like to destroy you, and those who despise you. They all fear you because they see the power of God working through you. They are like unto Saul and you are like David.

GOD SAYS TO YOU THIS DAY!

Ezekiel 3:17 (NLT)
"Son of man, I have appointed you as a watchman for Israel. Whenever you receive a message from me, pass it on to the people immediately."

As we dissect this and digest this a little bit at the time, we see Ezekiel being lifted physically by the Lord and transported to another location supernaturally. Sometimes God uses figurative examples to help us see what He is doing in us spiritually. We can relate to what we can see and what we know. God is using this illustration to show that this elevation was an act of His Spirit. It was God, Himself, lifting Ezekiel.

Psalms 75:6-7
"For promotion cometh neither from the east, nor from the west, nor from the south. But God is the judge: he putteth down one, and setteth up another. "

God makes it very clear when you are elevated to a new position. When you are promoted, it is He alone that promotes you. It is not because you were smarter. It is not because you worked harder. It is not because you know someone or you have a relative that pastors the church or owns the company. God makes it very clear that promotion comes from Him alone.

When God promotes, the angels rush in to see the wisdom of God and praise Him. The angels were eager to see whom God had selected for such a great and difficult task. There was such a throng of angels that were witness to his promotion. A great noise was made when their wings touched against one another as the crowd pushed in to see whom God selected. Ezekiel is made cognizant of this great assembly watching and praising God. It convinced and encouraged him of the greatness of his call. He received the strength of God to enable him to do that which He called him to do.

You see, Ezekiel's message was one of great difficulty, and yet greater deliverance and healing. Ezekiel was called to prophesy to those who were in captivity that they needed to repent and because they would not, even greater suffering was going to come upon them. Ezekiel prophesied the impending destruction of Jerusalem and the departure of God's glory from the temple because of the people's sins. He prophesied judgment to the false men and women prophets. He told of God's punishment for Israel for her idolatry. For years, Ezekiel prophesied destruction, lamentation, and doom and saw these things come to pass. Ezekiel was also the one who preached to the valley of dry bones and the restoration of Israel.

I can imagine that the people of Israel felt like, "We are the captives, the ones whom the Babylonians oppress and abuse. Why do we have to repent? They are the bad ones, not us." Often, when we are in pain from a wrong done to us, we cannot see our part in what caused it. Israel did not want to hear what Ezekiel had to say to them, and they wanted to kill him for even daring to ask them to repent.

From experience, I can tell you that promotion is not always the most pleasant experience. Don't misunderstand. Promotion is a blessing and a great responsibility, but it is not easy.

Ezekiel 3:14
"I went in bitterness, in the heat of my spirit; but the hand of the LORD was strong upon me."

Jesus Himself said, "Father, if it be thy will, let this cup pass from me." God, I don't want to do this. I don't want to go through the pain, suffering, and death. Nobody wants to go through that.

But the hand of the Lord was strong upon him and on you. The anointing is so strong that the Lord speaks to your heart with such a certainty that you know this is what you must do. God brings you to a place where you can say, like Jesus did, "Nevertheless, Not my will, but thy will be done."

Ezekiel was at his new position for seven days before he was even at a place emotionally where he could receive his orders. He sat in astonishment, emotionally incapable of even being told what his assignment was for seven days. Sometimes this happens. You come to yourself after a promotion, and you question yourself, "Did this really happen? Am I really here?" Fear grips you. The responsibility of what you have been called to do overwhelms you, and you haven't even been given specific instructions for your new position yet. Ezekiel sat in the presence of those in captivity, hearing their thoughts, getting to know them, and taking in what God would have him to speak to them. For seven days, he prepared his sermon.

God will send you to people in captivity, to Tel-Abib, to the hill of grain, a place in Babylon. The wheat has already been harvested. It is piled up into a hill of grain. He is not even sending you into the field to harvest. The grain has already been harvested and piled up in Babylon, this place of captivity. And this fruitful harvest is not just any old grain. This fruitful harvest is from Judah, which means praise. Our Savior is of the tribe of Judah. He is the Lion of Judah. He sends Ezekiel to God's people, besides the Chebar River.

Again, the Hebrew definition of (H3528) Chebar means a great while; long ago; length; already (seeing that which is now).

He leads us beside the still waters and restores our souls for a "great while." After a promotion, God knows your emotions need a restoration just from the move. You have been dislocated, and you need healing. It takes time to get your bearings on this new level. You don't know where to walk. You don't know what to do. You sit there, too astonished by the move to do anything. God knows it takes time by refreshing still waters to restore your turmoiled soul.

We are washed with the water of the WORD. God's WORD is a great river of water. Ezekiel sat by the River for seven days. We need to spend time in the WORD. Sometimes if we don't get revelation on a word right away, we move on. We won't wait for it. We must learn to wait by the river of living water until the WORD speaks to us; until we get an understanding of what God is saying to us.

Joshua 1:8 (NLT)
"Study this Book of Instruction continually. Meditate on it day and night so you will be sure to obey everything written in it. Only then will you prosper and succeed in all you do."

It was only then that God spoke to Ezekiel and told him that his purpose was to be a watchman on the wall to warn the people of their sin and to sound the alarm in Zion.

It is our job to speak to the prodigal son's, the woman caught in adultery, and to the Peters of the world.

Ezekiel was not called to speak to some foreign nation, but Israel. Ezekiel was called to preach to the church who had gone astray. The prodigal son is representative of a child who was raised in the right way but wanted to live his own way. The woman caught in adultery was a woman of Israel who was married to a man of the tribe of Israel. She knew the law and was, therefore, under the law and could be stoned for her sin. Peter was right there with Christ. These are the people you are called to minister to. That is part of what makes this ministry so difficult. The people in the world know their condition and will much more readily repent. Those in the church are much more difficult to minister to.

Speak to the prodigal sons who sometimes do some foolish things. He doesn't see things the way God does. He believes he knows more or he can do it better. The prodigal wants to get away from God's presence and live like he wants to live. He wants to party and enjoy life. He wastes his time, his youth, and his resources on foolish things, and sometimes our children do the same to us too. In these times, God allows the prodigal to come to the end of himself, the end of his resources, and the end of his jobs with no food- his spirit is empty. It is in this empty, broken place that God speaks to him through you. God speaks to the hurt and embarrassment. God speaks to the arrogance and insolence. He speaks to a heart that has realized that a mistake has been made and repentance needs to take place. God invites His children home through the words that He gives us to speak. We are whom He has elevated as His watchman.

God sees the prodigal son coming while he is still a long way off. He has not even come into God's presence yet in prayer. God welcomes and invites him to make a new beginning through the words that we speak.

As a watchman, we must speak to the woman caught in adultery as Jesus did.

John 8:4
"Teacher," they said to Jesus, "this woman was caught in the very act of adultery."

Sometimes life is very cruel. We end up caught up in things that we don't want to do, and we can't seem to get free. We get bound up in relationships and held captive by our emotions and our flesh. Sometimes we think we want to be there because, for a time, the pleasure of it soothes the pain of our broken hearts. Sometimes that bondage may not be a relationship. It may be an addiction to a substance, alcohol, tobacco, or drugs. When caught up in it, that "old friend" may help one to forget about the circumstances and numb the excruciating pain for a while. One's heart and spirit longs to be free, but one doesn't know any other way to escape the pain. One may try within him/herself to stop, promising themselves and others they will stop. But when life gets tough, or one feels lonely or depressed, one returns to that "old friend," or old habit, to seek solace, to escape the pain, to have some peace. For a time, the pain of loneliness and depression about the things of life seem to subside, but then one wakes-up and finds themselves in a place where their hearts don't want to be. They yearn to be free.

Others look on and judge. "She is caught in the very act. She is addicted to this lifestyle." I encourage you not to judge.

Most of us are caught up in some sort of addiction right now. That addiction might not be alcohol, tobacco, or drugs. That addiction may be to television, games, or an abusive relationship. That abuse may not be physical. That person may never hit you, but they do manipulate you in some manner. They control and dominate your life, and you are not free to be yourself. Your spirit feels trapped and smothered. You are caught in an addictive relationship. This addiction does not have to be a spouse or a boyfriend or a girlfriend. It may be with a parent or a sibling who was never there for you or never liked you — your soul and spirit thirst for their attention and their affection. One may continue to try to make things work in these relationships and nothing we ever do is good enough to win their love and attention. We end up devastated each time we try. We go away shattered, empty, and torn apart with pain inside. In time we come back to them again, seeking what we feel we need from them, only to be rejected again. This also is an addictive relationship. We are dependent on them for something they either cannot or chose not to give us.

The enemy plays on all of these types of situations. He accuses us and makes us feel guilty. He wants to keep us paralyzed and caught up in the guilt of not feeling worthy of forgiveness, much less worthy of doing anything for God. The enemy continually throws accusations and stones of guilt.

But God is a God of new beginnings. When He forgives us and set us free, He restores us to a place as if we have never done anything wrong.

As a watchman, we must speak these things and set captives free.

As a watchman, we must prophecy to the Peters of this world.

Matthew 26:34-35 (NLT)
"Peter," Jesus replied, "the truth is, this very night, before the rooster crows, you will deny me three times." "No!" Peter insisted. "Not even if I have to die with you! I will never deny you!" And all the other disciples vowed the same."

Some of us are like Peter. We have walked with the Lord for a while, and we love Him. We have seen Him perform miracles. He performed miracles in our personal lives, as He did with Peter when Jesus told him to drop his net to catch a multitude of fish; and when Jesus called him out of the boat and Peter walked on water in a storm. We have a great faith in Jesus. We impetuously defend Christ, as Peter did when he cut off the centurion's ear. Peter watched Jesus heal the sick, feed thousands, calm the raging sea, walk through walls, and disappear into the crowd so the enemy could not take him before his time. Peter knew the miracles God could do.

Yet when Jesus takes us to a place where we don't understand what He is doing, when He does not perform some great miracle of deliverance as we know He can, when Jesus seems to give Himself and us over to the enemy, we give up. We deny Jesus as Peter did. We might not say it with our mouths, but our actions speak volumes. We quit when it gets tough. We hide. We act like we don't know God or what to do. Out of fear, weariness, and confusion, we forget to pray. We forget to stand. We hide. We leave. We don't speak up. We don't want to die for someone else's sin. We want God to fix that other person or those people. We don't want to put up with the things that are wrong with them. We don't even want to be inconvenienced and annoyed or embarrassed because they don't know how to act. To repeat, we don't want to die for someone else's sin, and we don't understand why Christ would lead us to die, rather than just miraculously changing or fixing that person who is doing wrong.

We thought this would be a ministry of healing and miracles continuously. We thought Jesus would change the world and take over every evil place and bring His light, redemption, peace, and will. But we did not know we would have to put up with it. We never thought this would be a ministry of self-sacrifice and dying. And we run and hide. We stay home from church. We leave.

After Jesus' death and resurrection, Peter and the others repented for their attitudes and their actions. God forgave them and restored them, these same ones who denied Jesus and ran and hid when it was time to die.

Because of Jesus' resurrection from the dead and impartation of the Holy Spirit, these same ones experienced a time of new beginnings. They became the foundation of the church as we know it today. There has to be death, burial and resurrection, before there can be new life. As a leader, you must walk through this experience.

As a prophet, and as a leader over whatever and whomever God has called you to, we must pronounce judgment and destruction for a time. Too often, when God sends a warning, we try to rescue and fix things. We must learn to let go and let God have His perfect work in every situation. This is especially hard with our children and families. We don't want to see them suffer, and sometimes, we are a safety net for all of their mistakes. We perpetuate and prolong their sins and mistakes when we do not allow them to undergo judgment.

As a prophet, and as a leader over whatever and whomever God has called you to, it is so important that like Ezekiel, after the judgment and death, you speak to the valley of dry bones. You MUST prophesy over all the dead, dry places. You must speak over your MINISTRY, your children, your family, YOUR LIFE, your finances, the NATIONS, and the SYSTEMS you have been called to -- whatever is dead and not producing. Speak as the LORD gives you direction. It is a process. While things are still looking dead and hopeless, you must speak to it. While it appears that things can never come back together again, you must speak to it. When it appears that this body will never come together, you must speak to it. The bondage that people have been in may be as strong and cruel as the grave. They may have been held captive there until all hope was lost and nothing was left but dry bones. Only God can make these bones live. Prophecy to the bones.

Ezekiel 37:4-6
"O ye dry bones, hear the word of the LORD. Thus saith the Lord God unto these bones; Behold, I will cause breath to enter into you, and ye shall live: And I will lay sinews upon you, and will bring up flesh upon you, and cover you with skin, and put breath in you, and ye shall live; and ye shall know that I am the LORD."

And as you watch things begin to come back together again, prophecy to the wind, to the precious Holy Spirit.

Ezekiel 37:9
"Thus saith the Lord God; Come from the four winds, O breath, and breathe upon these slain, that they may live."

God can fix the most hopeless of situations. HE WILL RESTORE LIFE, where it appeared so hopeless. This is your mission. This is your call.

JUST AS SURELY AS God physically lifted EZEKIEL and transported him to another location, supernaturally God has lifted you to your new position to fulfill your promotion. WALK INTO THIS

NEW POSITION, THIS NEW LEVEL, AND BRING GLORY GOD!!!

In this book, SEE IT, THINK IT, SAY IT, WRITE, BELIEVE IT, BE IT, information is shared to explain the process of preparation for the things that God has planned for your life. Also, this book will help you to identify your purpose, stay on path, and learn how to accomplish the vision that God has placed in your heart.

CHAPTER ONE

SEE IT

Genesis 1:26 (NLT)
Then God said, "Let us make human beings in our image, to be like us. They will reign over the fish in the sea, the birds in the sky, the livestock, all the wild animals on the earth, and the small animals that scurry along the ground."

Deuteronomy 28:13
And the Lord will make you the head and not the tail; you shall be above only, and not be beneath, if you heed the commandments of the Lord your God, which I command you today, and are careful to observe them.

Romans 5:17
"For if by the one mans' offense death reigned through the one, much more those who receive abundance of grace and the gift of righteousness will reign in life through the One, Jesus Christ."

- God makes it clear in these Scriptures that we are to reign in life. To reign is to rule or have dominion.

- To reign is to lead. In order to lead, one must have vision. One must SEE IT. Without vision, one is just a manager, maintaining the day-to-day operations of someone else's vision.

- Vision and our foundation are tied together.

Some people invent things to do or join in with others who are doing a good thing but not necessarily a God thing, because they do not hear clearly from God, and they feel they should be doing something. Churches are full of people who jump into 'helps' ministries for the sake of doing something good because others are telling them that this is what they are supposed to do. It may not be at all what God created them to do.

Sometimes we cannot see at all, or we cannot see clearly what God would have us to do, because there are issues in our foundation or sin in our lives blinding us or blocking our view.

We must seek God concerning these issues, repent, and receive forgiveness.

JOSEPH REIGNED

Joseph had dreams as a boy of others bowing to him. He knew in his heart at an early age that it was his destiny to rule and reign. Joseph loved the Lord and was an obedient son.

DAVID REIGNED

David was anointed to be king by the prophet Samuel when he was just a boy. He spent time with God and worshipped God on the backside of the mountain while he tended his father's sheep.

While guarding his father's sheep, David learned, by the power of God, how to kill a lion and a bear as a boy. Those victories gave him courage and grace to face Goliath and defeat him.

Gideon Reigned- Esther Reigned- Daniel Reigned

Each had a strong relationship with God and sought God's wisdom, grace, and power to achieve their purposes. If one studies the lives of each of these people, one can see that each one loved and respected God greatly. Their foundations were solid in God. They were obedient to God's will, even when they were mistreated and lied upon. Even though each went through terrible trials, each demonstrated their respect of the Lord, and they put God first above all else. They demonstrated knowledge of God's Word, and they walked it out in their lives.

John 17:19
"And for their sakes I sanctify myself, that they also may be sanctified by the truth."

Philippians 2:12
"Therefore, my beloved, as you have always obeyed, not as in my presence only, but now much more in my absence, work out your own salvation with fear and trembling."

We have a responsibility to sanctify ourselves so that we can bring others to Christ and not cause others to stumble. Godly fear equips us to handle abundance, resources, and wealth properly.

Proverbs 10:22 (NKJV)
"The blessings of the Lord makes one rich, And He adds no sorrow to with it."

Each of us must be willing to sacrifice our vision to the will of God. We must love God even more than our purpose.

Genesis 22:3
" So Abraham rose early in the morning and saddled his donkey, and took two of his young men with him, and Isaac his son; and he split the wood for the burnt offering, and arose and went to the place of which God had told him."

Obedience is the outward evidence of the true fear of God and a true love of God.

We must obey God; immediately. When we don't understand, even if it is painful and we do not see the benefit, continue until it is finished.

Genesis 22:12
And He said, "Do not lay your hand on the lad or do anything to him: for I know that you fear God, since you have not withheld your son, your only son from Me."

I went through this process:

- I gave up a possible career as a doctor and left family and school (1974)
- I left the classroom, my students, and my programs to become an assistant principal (1995).
- I left that school to become a principal (2000).
- We left our children, our church and ministry, our home, my school, my career in education to move to Virginia Beach as directed by God (2005).
- We moved to Suffolk, again, as directed by God (2016).

1 Peter 1:7 (paraphrased)
The testing of your faith is more precious than gold.

(Paraphrased from Romans 5:8-10)
GOD DEMONSTRATED HIS GREAT LOVE FOR US IN THAT HE GAVE HIS SON, HIS ONLY SON, SO THAT WE MAY HAVE THE RIGHT TO ETERNAL LIFE.

To be most effective, God requires us to give Him our all, as He did for us. We must spend more time with Him to receive that grace, strength, and power.

Sometimes we only see a little because we are trying to operate in our strength, rather than trusting God to do "exceedingly abundantly above what we can ask or think."

Sometimes we only see a little because we fail to act on what we do see.

When I first started teaching in high school, I did not understand how to accomplish what God was telling me to do. The Principal came to me one day and asked me to serve on a committee to improve student performance and increase minority participation in honors-level classes. Little by little, God would reveal things and ideas to me. As I implemented each step, God would give me more.

We initiated a program called Models and Mentors (M&M) for the young men and Self Esteem Enhancement (SEE) for the young ladies. These programs were designed to help students feel more a part of the school. They had a place to belong and grow. A separate class called Academic Plus (A+), designed to help prepare minority students for honors-level classes, grew from these ideas. Ideas for the classes; training in the four major subjects; business site visits and tours; guest speakers; college tours; an end of the year awards/scholarship dinner ceremony; and more grew from that as we walked out each phase. I did not get the whole vision all at once. It came through time as I implemented and walked in what I did see. Night by night, God would speak to my heart and give me visions and dreams of the next steps or things to add and what to look out for. The program was a huge success only because I did it God's way. Each of those students went on to do amazing things. I give God all the glory. I still keep in contact with some of my students. It is joy and such a privilege to walk and work with God and witness His amazing power.

We must seek God for the wisdom to rule and reign. Our foundation must be solid. Our discernment must be intact because the enemy will try to tempt us with things that look good.

Job 22:28 NKJV
You shall declare a thing and it shall be established for you, So light will shine on your way.

As we declare things in prayer, God gives us direction. We can see clearly which way to go and what to do.

There is more than one way to declare a thing. A declaration is not just a verbal thing. The Declaration of Independence is a written document.

A written plan is a declaration of what you plan to do.

Architects draw out plans long before the first brick is laid.

Scientists write out chemical formulas for products that they create. God gave us a written plan of how to live in the Bible.

Habakkuk 2:2
Write the vision and make it plain on tablets, that he may run who reads it.

Good leaders write out plans so others can know what to do and how to do it. Policy and procedures, if done well, always make the work easier, more efficient, and prevent misunderstandings. They provide guidelines for the work and resolutions when there is trouble.

If we do not love God more than our purpose or our vision, we will be tempted to sacrifice our integrity, choosing what looks good and miss God, thus losing our witness.

THE WHOLE PURPOSE OF EVERY VISION IS TO BRING GLORY TO GOD! as described in Luke 4:18 (NKJV):

"The Spirit of the Lord is upon Me,
Because He has anointed Me
To preach the gospel to the poor;
He has sent Me to heal the brokenhearted,
To proclaim liberty to the captives

And recovery of sight to the blind,
To set at liberty those who are oppressed;
To proclaim the acceptable year of the Lord."

I shared a portion of what that of vision looked like for me in education. Each of you should have a vision of what God has called you to do in the sphere where you reign.

WRITE OUT YOUR VISION FROM GOD.

I would not trade my experience with God through that time as an educator and co-pastor for anything. To have the experience of walking and working with God and watching Him do the miraculous is invaluable. I am so grateful to be used by God. My call was and still is to restore sight to the blind, to set the captives free, and be a prophet to the nations. (Jeremiah 1:5)

God wants us to give Him our weaknesses, failures, talents, strengths, and let Him use them for His Glory!

God desires to reign over our inner life-our will, emotions, desires, and thoughts. As we learn to take every thought captive to the obedience of Christ, we will learn how to take dominion in the earth. For it is in the mind, will, emotions, desires, and thoughts that the enemy controls the world and takes them captive. Thank God that HE has given us authority and power over all the power of the enemy through His Word, by the power of the Holy Spirit, and Jesus' shed blood. I will speak frequently about taking dominion in the earth. It was God's plan in the beginning, and He sent Jesus to restore us to that original place as His sons and daughters. We are to walk in the dominion on the earth that Jesus won back for us. We must learn to fight using spiritual warfare through God's strength and glory!!! SEE IT! See the plan God has for your life.

Ephesians 1:18-19 (NKJV)
[18] the eyes of your [a]understanding being enlightened; that you may know what is the hope of His calling, what are the riches of the glory of His inheritance in the saints, [19] and what is the exceeding greatness of His power toward us who believe, according to the working of His mighty power

CHAPTER TWO

THINK IT

Romans 12:2
…be ye transformed by the renewing of your mind, that ye may prove what is that good , and acceptable, and perfect will of God.

One's thought process is a critical element in transformation.

Romans 8:5 (AMP)
"For those who are according to the flesh and are controlled by its unholy desires set their minds on and pursue those things which gratify the flesh, but those who are according to the Spirit and are controlled by the desires of the Spirit set their minds on and seek those things which gratify the [Holy] Spirit."

The greatest hindrance that keeps us from becoming all that God has for us to become is fear. Fear about one's unworthiness, fear about one's inabilities, and fear about what others will say, or have said, and think about us. Our parents or teachers may have said to us, "You will never be anything." Or, we may have been passed over at work again and again for promotion because our supervisor may not have felt we were capable. That very act of denial of the position spoke a lie into our spirit that holds us captive.

God desires to do a healing and setting free in us regarding how and what we think about ourselves and the plans God has for our lives.

Remember the 12 men of Israel who went and spied out the land. All but Joshua and Caleb saw themselves as grasshoppers compared to the giants in the land, and most of Israel feared to go in and take what God had promised to them because the Reproach (curse) of Slavery was upon them. The way they thought about themselves kept them from receiving the promises of God.

Reproach is another word for shame.

Shame is defined as disappointed, delayed, frustrated or confused, to condemn to an unhappy fate, to criticize adversely, to cause the ruin of, make fail, to feel unworthy, disgrace, taunt, and rail.

The Israelites saw themselves as not worthy to receive the blessings God had in store for them. Because they feared, they did not enter into the Promised Land, but their children did.

How many of us see ourselves as not worthy of becoming all that God has for us because of something that we did in the past or something that someone did or said to us that made us feel unworthy? That feeling of unworthiness creates a fear within us. Because of this fear, we keep ourselves from receiving the blessings that God has for us.

Ephesians 1:4-5 (NIV)
"Just as He chose us in Him before the foundation of the world, that we should be holy and without blame before Him in love, 5 having predestined us to adoption as sons by Jesus Christ to Himself"

James 1:5 (NKJV)
"If any of you lacks wisdom, let him ask of God, who gives to all liberally and without reproach, and it will be given to him."

In the past, God dealt with me about not wanting to receive a promotion He ordained for me and not taking advantage of healing prayer that He provided for me because I felt unworthy to receive it. I repented for this.

Remember Gideon, who thought of himself as the least of the least and was hiding in the winepress in fear when God called him a "mighty man of valor." God knew who Gideon was before he was born. That is why he was named GIDEON, which means, "mighty warrior."

From Joshua 5, we see that it was in Gilgal that God rolled away the Reproach of Slavery from Israel. This transformation was necessary before they could defeat the seven nations and possess the Promised Land.

And remember David, who was hiding in fear in the cave of Adullam - the place of the squeeze, with everyone who was in debt and distress and everyone who was in despair (1 Samuel 22).

It was in this place, that God told David to arise and take the throne as king in Judah.

God strengthens us to rise and take our places as kings and priests while we are yet in the place of fear, shame, despair, debt, and distress. Only God can transform us in this way, as we are obedient to Him.

This is the fire of transformation. We are purified and transformed in the heat, as silver or gold is purified in the fire. God will turn up the heat to provide the correct environment for our transformation. This change in us is necessary to bring glory to God.

As others realize, through what they see us go through in our lives, we serve the true and living God, they are drawn to God by our brave response.

Shadrach, Meshach, and Abednego had their minds set to serve only the true and living God. Gideon had his mind set to do what God told him to do. The children of the Israelites had their minds set to serve the true and living God.

Is your thought process set to the point that you are willing to die to complete what God has for you to do?

Have you ever been in a situation at work where you were doing the right thing, and people conspired against you to get rid of you because they were jealous? Some would fight back. Some would complain to their boss or supervisor.

Instead, Shadrach, Meshach, and Abednego responded with these words when they were brought before the king by jealous people:

Daniel 3:17-18 (AMPC)
"If our God whom we serve is able to deliver us from the burning fiery furnace, He will deliver us out of your hand, O king.
 But if not, let it be known to you, O king, that we will not serve your gods or worship the golden image which you have set up!"

Their minds were set on serving the true and living God.

Because of what God did with them in the fire, this ungodly king acknowledged that their God was "the true and living God."

In job situations, some may have thought, and even said to God, "God, You are going to change my bosses mind and cause him or her to see the light, before he/she fires me, right?"

Like Shadrach, Meshach, and Abednego, we may have to walk through the fire. God does not want us to panic in the situation. God wants us to be assured that He will provide for us no matter what happens. We will be tested to trust God no matter what things look like.

Repenting and asking for forgiveness for believing the lies of the enemy is the first thing that we must do to be delivered from the fear that once controlled us.

Gideon tore down the altar of Baal and asked for forgiveness and repented for the sins of his fathers (Ancestors) and himself as part of his deliverance and transformation. In this manner, Gideon broke the curse that was upon him and Israel for their sin of serving other gods.

Generations before entering the Promised Land, the people of Israel came to Egypt because of a severe famine in their land. While in Egypt, they forgot who they were and whose they were. They saw themselves as less than children of God. This sin opened the door to the enemy. Even though they were great in number, because of how they saw themselves, they allowed themselves to become slaves. That slave mentality carried a curse, which passed through the generations.

While Israel was at Gilgal, the men were circumcised and they celebrated the Passover.

These two acts were symbolic of what Jesus does for us. They did these acts, and God broke the curse of slavery that was upon them.

Romans 2:29 (NLT)
... a true Jew is one whose heart is right with God. And true circumcision is not a cutting of the body but a change of heart produced by God's Spirit. Whoever has that kind of change seeks praise from God, not from people.

The Passover is a seven-day process that celebrates the deliverance of the tribes of Israel from Egypt. They were set free from the bondage that enslaved them.

Colossians 2:11-15 (AMP)
In Him also you were circumcised with a circumcision not made with hands, but in a [spiritual] circumcision [performed by] Christ by stripping off the body of the flesh (the whole corrupt, carnal nature with its passions and lusts).
[12][Thus you were circumcised when] you were buried with Him in [your] baptism, in which you were also raised with Him to a new life] through [your] faith in the working of God [as displayed] when He raised Him from the dead.
[13]And you who were dead in trespasses and in the uncircumcision of your flesh (your sensuality, your sinful carnal nature), [God] brought to life together with [Christ], having [freely] forgiven us all our transgressions,

¹⁴Having canceled and blotted out and wiped away the handwriting of the note (bond) with its legal decrees and demands, which was in force and stood against us (hostile to us). This [note with its regulations, decrees, and demands] He set aside and cleared completely out of our way by nailing it to [His] cross. (The curses were broken)

¹⁵[God] disarmed the principalities and powers that were ranged against us and made a bold display and public example of them, in triumphing over them in Him and in it [the cross]. "

The generation that crossed the Jordan River into the Promised Land had never been slaves in Egypt. They had strong faith in God, believing that HE would take them across an impassable flood.

They believed that God would give them victory over the giants in the land who were bigger and stronger than they were, as they were obedient to God.

They believed that God would grant them full possession of the Promised Land and the great and precious promises of God.

They believed many great things, and yet, they carried the reproach of slavery in Egypt.

They were in the Promised Land, yet they carried a curse; a curse that prevented them from being able to take possession of the promises of God. THEY CARRIED THE REPROACH OF SLAVERY IN EGYPT EVEN THOUGH THEY HAD NEVER BEEN SLAVES.

They were saved, yet they were not able to possess and become all that God had for them because a curse was preventing them from possessing it; just as a curse may be preventing us from becoming all that God has for us.

The reproach of slavery carries a spirit of poverty and a curse. The curse was passed from their forefathers to them. While in this state, God had to give them food to survive, just enough for that day because when someone is bound in slavery and poverty, one has difficulty managing wealth. There is a tendency to want to keep all one can get for oneself because there is a fear of not having enough for tomorrow. There is a fear of having lack again. Because a person in this state holds on to all he/she can get, he/she cannot allow the blessings of wealth to flow through them as a conduit. They cannot be a channel of blessing. Survival is the main thought.

Once the reproach of slavery is rolled away, the curse is broken, and one's thinking changes. One can find wealth all around. There is no fear of lack. One can see how to prosper. One can be a channel of blessing. One sows and reaps bountifully. There is boldness instead of fear. One possesses the power and the authority to take dominion.

Because the children of Israel performed circumcisions and celebrated the Passover, the curse was broken.

One of the things that God dealt with Gideon about was trusting in God rather than himself or man's way of doing things. God pared-down Gideon's army of thousands down to 300 to face 135,000 enemy troops. He was instructed to go into this battle with trumpets and pitchers with torches in them. This is foreign to man's way of thinking. We must learn to see things from God's perspective.

The children of Israel, Gideon, David and Shadrach, Meshach, and Abednego chose to do things God's way - NOT man's way.

Romans 12:2 (AMP)
We are "transformed" as we "renew our minds" on the Word of God, so that we can prove what is the good and acceptable and perfect will of God, even the thing that is good and acceptable and perfect [in His sight for you.]

2 Timothy 1:7(NKJV)
"For God has not given us a spirit of fear, but of power and of love and of a sound mind."

1 John 4:18 (NKJV)
"There is no fear in love; but perfect love casts out fear, because fear involves torment. But he who fears has not been made perfect (mature) in love."

Proverbs 12:25 (NKJV)
"Anxiety (which is a form of fear) in the heart of man causes depression, but a good word makes it glad."

Psalm 119:93 (TLB)
"I will never forget your commandments. You have used them to restore my joy and my health."

Nehemiah 8:10 (NKJV)
"The joy of the Lord is your strength."

Isaiah 12:3 (AMP)
"With joy, we draw water from the wells of salvation."

The Spirit of Joy that God gives us allows us to be nourished by the Water of God's Word.

Deuteronomy 8:3 (AMP)
"And He humbled you and allowed you to hunger and fed you with manna, which you did not know nor did your fathers know, that He might make you recognize and personally know that man does not live by bread only, but man lives by every word that proceeds out of the mouth of the Lord."

The bread of life causes us to recognize and personally know that man lives by every word that proceeds from the mouth of God. We need God's word to become a part of us to live the Kingdom life that God has planned for us.

Psalm 119:11 (NKJV)
"Thy Word have I hid in my heart that I might not sin against thee."

When one hides something in one's heart, one more than memorizes it; it becomes a part of them.

We are to "Think It," meditate on the Word constantly. It is there that we learn and gain the wisdom to become prosperous and successful in the things of God.

Joshua 1:8 (NKJV)
"This Book of the Law shall not depart out of your mouth, but you shall meditate on it day and night,

that you may observe and do according to all that is written in it. For then you shall make your way prosperous, and then you shall deal wisely and have good success."

Psalm 139:23-24 (NKJV)
"23 Search me, O God, and know my heart;
Try me, and know my anxieties;
24 And see if there is any wicked way in me, And lead me in the way everlasting."

We must ask God to reveal the deep and hidden things: the wounds and lies that cause the fears and anxieties in our hearts that hold us in bondage.

We must boldly declare the truth of God's Word over those lies so our thinking can be transformed. Then, we must ask God and allow Him to lead us out of bondage.

Philippians 4:6-8 (NKJV)
"6 Be anxious for nothing, but in everything by prayer and supplication, with thanksgiving, let your requests be made known to God; 7 and the peace of God, which surpasses all understanding, will guard your hearts and minds through Christ Jesus... Meditate on These Things."

As we ask God about these fears and anxieties and give them to God, His peace will guard our hearts and minds through Christ Jesus. God instructs us to meditate - think again and again on these things.

"Think about it." As we ask God about these fears and anxieties and give them to Him. His peace will guard our hearts and minds through Christ Jesus.

Guard your heart!

Proverbs 4:23 (NIV)
"Above all else, guard your heart, for everything you do flows from it."

Your heart controls your thoughts. Your thoughts control your actions.

Before a person can do a thing, a person must first "think it."

God instructs us on how to grow further and receive greater revelation and more understanding about the things that He has for us. The enemy would have us to think negative things about ourselves and what we are unable to do. God instructs us to think about the good things He has for us.

Philippians 4:8 (NKJV)
"Finally, brethren, whatever things are true, whatever things are noble, whatever things are just, whatever things are pure, whatever things are lovely, whatever things are of good report, if there is any virtue and if there is anything praiseworthy—meditate on these things."

If thoughts that come into your mind that do not qualify with the Word in Phil 4, take it captive, according to 2 Corinthians 10:5.

"Casting down arguments and every high thing that exalts itself against the knowledge of God, bringing every thought into captivity to the obedience of Christ. "

Then, give those thoughts to God, and He will give you His peace and guard your heart and mind.

Learn how to cast your cares on Jesus and win the war on worry and fear.

We are to pray for one another regarding our identity and destiny in Christ. God wants us to know that He gives us His wisdom and understanding and power so that we can be very fruitful and successful in what He has plat for us to do.

Colossians 1:9-11 (NIV)
"9 For this reason, since the day we heard about you, we have not stopped praying for you. We continually ask God to fill you with the knowledge of his will through all the wisdom and understanding that the Spirit gives, 10 so that you may live a life worthy of the Lord and please him in every way: bearing fruit in every good work, growing in the knowledge of God, 11being strengthened with all power according to his glorious might so that you may have great endurance and patience "

God gives us His Spirit of self-control so that we will have the discipline necessary to stay on track, train, and prepare our minds and bodies to complete all that He has for us to do.

Galatians 5:23 (NIV)
"But the fruit of the Spirit is .... self-control."

Isaiah 10:27
"And the Yoke was destroyed because of the anointing."

God wants us to know that the yoke of fear that held us in bondage is destroyed by the anointing.

As the ox ate some of the very grain he was treading, he began to grow fatter. As we eat and digest more and more of the Word, the anointing grows. The neck of the oxen grew so fat that the yoke was broken off of his neck. Likewise, the yoke of the enemy is broken off of our necks because of the anointing of the Holy Spirit and the fatness of God's Word in us, which transforms us.

Mark 4:24 (AMP)
" And He said to them, Be careful what you are hearing. The measure [of thought and study] you give [to the truth you hear] will be the measure [of virtue and knowledge] that comes back to you—and more [besides] will be given to you who hear."

The word, virtue, in this Scripture means, "dunamis power."

Strong's Concordance defines the word "Dunamis" (1411) as miraculous power, force, ability, might, excellence. It is also where we get the word, dynamite, which has explosive power. It is the same word used where Jesus said He felt "virtue" go out of Him when He was touched in faith by the women with the issue of blood.

Great anointing and power comes upon us as we think about and study God's Word concerning the things that He has for us!

So, in conclusion, confess the sin of believing the lies of the enemy rather than the truth of God's Word and for living our lives according to these lies rather than the truth.

Forgive our ancestors and parents who have passed down these ungodly beliefs to us and any others who have passed down these wrong beliefs to us, such as teachers, bosses, and friends, siblings, and spouses.

Repent for yourself and our ancestors. Ask God's forgiveness for living a life based on these untruths and begin to live a life based on who God says we are.

Forgive yourself for making these mistakes.

Renounce these wrong beliefs and break its power over your life based on the finished work of Jesus Christ.

Declare what God says in His Word, rather than the lies of the enemy. Take every thought captive.

Think about yourself as the person God created to meet the specific need that He has placed on your heart. Be flexible enough to flow with God to increase and grow. God loves you, and He wants to set you free to become all that He has for you, so that you might bring Him great glory!

THINK IT!!!

CHAPTER THREE

SAY IT

Job 22:28 (NKJV)
You shall declare a thing and it shall be established for you. So light will shine your way.

Everything in the universe begins with and revolves around two things: thoughts and words. God spoke, and the worlds were framed by His Words.

YOU MUST SAY A THING IN FAITH FOR IT TO COME TO PASS.

Dr. Trimm stated, "Your thoughts, ideas, words, and prayers have massive power to mold and engineer your current and future existence. Your spiritual genes hold the creative power to frame your personal world by the thoughts and words you think and speak, which are divine tools given for your creative use."

Much of what we experience and ultimately achieve can be traced back to how we have made use of these two simple, yet vastly powerful tools- our words and our thoughts.

That is why Proverbs tells us, "For as he thinks in his heart, so is he" (Proverbs 23:7 AMP) and urges us to "guard your heart above all else, for it determines the course of your life." (Proverbs 4:23 NLT)

Jesus said, "Whatever is in your heart determines what you say." or [Out of the abundance of the heart the mouth speaks]. (Matthew 12:34 NKJV)

A good person produces good things from the treasury of a good heart, and an evil person produces evil things from the treasury of an evil heart. (Matthew 12:35 NLT)

What occupies our minds determines what will eventually come out of our mouths. It is imperative that we understand the nature of what we are thinking, and it is most important that we become the master of our thoughts and speech.

WHAT WE SAY EVEN DETERMINES OUR OWN SALVATION.

Romans 10:10 (NKJV)
For with the heart man believes unto righteousness, and with the mouth confession is made unto salvation.!!!!

It is not until we SAY IT that we receive salvation. God instructed Joshua to meditate on His Word day and night so that it would fill his heart, mind, and mouth. Then he commanded him to be strong and of good courage.

Until Joshua's mind and mouth thought and spoke God's Word, only then could Joshua have any hope of being strong and courageous.

Joshua 1:8-9 (AMPC)
This Book of the Law shall not depart out of your mouth, (meaning you should never stop saying it) but you shall meditate on it day and night, that you may observe and do according to all that is written in it. For then you shall make your way prosperous, and then you shall deal wisely and have good success.

Have not I commanded you? Be strong, and very courageous. Be not afraid, neither be dismayed, for the Lord your God is with you wherever you go.

From the outset, God made it a priority to address the issue of Joshua's mind. No other instructions took precedence over what occupied Joshua's thoughts. One's thoughts impact one's heart. Again, "out of the abundance of the heart the mouth speaks."

Only as we "SAY IT" in faith will things come to pass.
We can only "SAY IT" in faith if we first believe it in our hearts.
It is necessary to SAY IT!
It is only as we "SAY IT" (The Vision) that we begin to demonstrate our faith for the vision.
It is only as we "SAY IT" (The Vision) that God is activated to do it.

In order for Joshua to lead the people of Israel to take possession of the Promised Land, God had to deal with Joshua's heart and mind, so that what came out of his mouth was only faith-filled words of what God said He would do. This was necessary because the giants in the Promised Land were bigger and stronger than the people of Israel. The things that God told the people of Israel to do were humanly impossible. Only as Joshua spoke in faith was he able to be courageous. Scripture tells us that God watches over His word to perform it.

Jeremiah 1:11,12 (AMP)
God asked Jeremiah, what do you see? Jeremiah responded,
[11] I see a branch or shoot of an almond tree [the emblem of alertness and activity, blossoming in late winter].
[12] Then said the Lord to me, You have seen well, for I am alert and active, watching over My word to perform it.

As we speak in agreement with what God's Word says, we can be assured that He will do it.

God spoke through Isaiah saying, "So shall My word be that goes forth from My mouth; It shall not return to Me void, But it shall accomplish what I please, And it shall prosper in the thing for which I sent it (Isaiah 55:11 NKJV).

God instructs us to speak what His Word says regarding the things that He desires for us to do, no matter how things appear.

God may tell us to do things that seem impossible with man, but ALL things are possible with God.

Too often, what is in our hearts and what comes out of our mouths are controlled by what we see and experience, rather than by what God's Word says because our thoughts are not God's thoughts.

We are to have the mind of Christ. How do we do this? We must spend time in the Word and allow the Word to work in us. God's Word is alive and powerful, and we are transformed as we renew our minds on the Word of God.

In addition, pray in the Spirit. As we pray in the Spirit, the Holy Spirit helps us in our weaknesses and prays for us according to the will of God.

Filter out anything that you do not want to present itself in your future and focus on what God truly desires you to have.

God has taught us to think as he thinks as we take hold of His Word.

Philippians 4:6-8 (NKJV)
[6] Be anxious for nothing, but in everything by prayer and supplication, with thanksgiving, let your requests be made known to God; [7] and the peace of God, which surpasses all understanding, will guard your hearts and minds through Christ Jesus. [8] Finally, brethren, whatever things are true, whatever things are noble, whatever things are just, whatever things are pure, whatever things are lovely, whatever things are of

good report, if there is any virtue and if there is anything praiseworthy—meditate on these things.

This tells us NOT to be anxious about anything and to fix our thoughts on what is true, noble, just, pure, lovely, of good report, virtuous, and praiseworthy. This is the way God thinks.

It is important to be intentional about what we see and hear because it will have a great impact on what we think. People are flooded with violence and corruption and all manner of wrong thinking as they watch TV, iPads, phones, and computers. Businesses know that what people see and hear will form an impression in their minds. Before people realize it, they are thinking and saying what the commercials say, and then they are acting upon those thoughts. That is why there are so many commercials on television. Businesses know that what people see and hear in the commercials influence human behavior. People will be out there buying that BigMac that they don't need and the food processor that they don't want because it was imprinted on their minds by a commercial that they heard and saw. The programs we watch have a similar impact on our hearts and minds. We must be careful what we allow through our eye and ear gates, and we must guard our hearts.

SEE IT, THINK IT, SAY IT, WRITE IT • 55

The enemy is constantly whispering lies into our minds and flashing scenes of past memories he wants to keep in our minds to get us to say what he wants us to say and do what he wants us to do.

Joyce Meyer wrote a book entitled Battlefield of the Mind. One of the chapters is entitled "Wilderness Mentalities." In this book, she states that there are certain thought patterns that we can have that keep us in the wilderness, walking around the same mountain-the same mindset- again and again. Israel had a mountain of fear and rebellion that kept them walking around the same mountain for 40 years, staying in the same place doing the same thing, unable to possess the Promised Land. God will allow us to stay right there until we learn to change the way we think about things and learn to see things and think about things the way God does. This is because our thoughts will determine what we say, and what we say will determine our actions and our outcome.

We must learn to tell that mountain "be removed and be cast into the sea."

Many people believe that their future is determined by their past and present. They stay right there, doing the same things that have always done.

Some may want another person to do things for them because they don't want to take responsibility.

I once had a staff member who had a very prominent role in the school. She had a good idea for a special "school within a school," where the school day was extended to increase learning time, and students wore uniforms. This was a tested program that had been successful in other places. This staff member supported me in receiving my job at this school. Little did I know that her plan was for me to run this special "school within a school." Well, God had already given me His plan for the entire school, but I was not opposed to this person running this "school within a school" herself since it was her vision. I lent my support and encouragement for her to do so, but, she was not happy. She wanted me to do it for her. She did not want to take responsibility.

Others believe that if a thing is God's will for them to do, it will be easy.

Nehemiah would never have finished the wall around Jerusalem if he did not persevere under persecution and difficulty. David would never have become King if he had given up while in the Cave of Adullam.

Others may feel that they are not worthy.

That was Gideon's problem, initially.

Some just want to do things their way.
This was King Saul's problem.

These and many other mindsets will keep us from reaching our destinies.

How are mindsets torn down or removed? Mindsets are removed as we bring our thoughts captive to the obedience of Christ. God teaches us to war in the spirit with His Word by taking every thought that we have or that the enemy places in our minds and answer it, cast it down, and bring it into captivity by aligning our thoughts with the Word of God and speaking to it. We must SAY IT. We must say what the Word of God says about our situation.

When we feel as if we are wandering in the dark and cannot figure out what to do, we should stop and give this command: "Let there be light." God will begin to show us what to do. He will give us wisdom and understanding if we will ask Him. This is why we declare revelation Scriptures over ourselves, and this church frequently.

God tells in Proverbs to, "Get wisdom! Get understanding! Do not forget, nor turn away from the words of my mouth. Do not forsake her, and she will preserve you; Love her, and she will keep you. Wisdom is the principal thing; Therefore get wisdom. And in all your getting, get understanding." (Proverbs 4:5-7 NKJV)

It is very important to not only have "the what," but also "the why, when, where, and how." Only God can answer those questions.

As a kingdom principle, God has designed each of us to create Godly success and abundance in every sphere we influence, and we do this by what we think, which produces what we say.

We have been tasked with taking Kingdom dominion in the area where God has assigned us. The vision He has given us is for that purpose. Jesus came that we might have life and that we might have it more abundantly for the purpose of Kingdom dominion.

Again, WHAT WE THINK Determines WHAT WE SAY, which will influence WHAT WE DO.

As I stated in Chapter 1, the principal came to me to ask me to work with a group of teachers and supporting staff on a program to improve student academic performance and increase minority participation in Honors Level classes. We initiated a program and talked with school officials about our plans. We talked with business and community leaders about what we hoped to accomplish, then we talked to parents, and finally, we talked with the students about this program. Much thought and prayer went into this vision, but before anything could happen, we had to talk about it. We had to SAY IT.

It is necessary to tell someone about your vision. My experience has been to pray it first, then say it to others.

In Genesis 41, Joseph prayed, and God gave him the vision to interpret the dream and the plan to prepare for the future. In a time of famine, (great lack), all of Israel was taken care of with great abundance. The rest of the world would come to them to buy grain just to live.

God wants us to prepare for a future of great abundance in a time of lack.

Genesis 47:6 (NKJV)
"To dwell in the best of the land. Let them live in the land of Goshen."

Moses prayed, and God gave him the plan and set the stage for Israel's deliverance from bondage. God set Israel free and gave them the wealth of Egypt as they left. Moses said to Pharaoh, "Let my people go."

Joshua prayed, and God gave him the plan to win each battle, to possess the Promised Land, and receive the wealth contained in it.

Nehemiah prayed to restore and rebuild the walls of Jerusalem (the walls of the church), and God provided great wealth to complete the task and to restore Israel.

Esther prayed, and God gave her the plan for the deliverance of Israel.

Daniel read the book of the law and saw the future. He began to pray for that future of the deliverance and restoration of Israel.

Peter and John prayed then three thousand souls were saved and gave so that there was no lack among any of the believers. Again they prayed then five thousand more were saved and they gave and had all things in common, and the ministry of the church was funded.

WE MUST SAY IT. WE MUST GIVE A POSITIVE CONFESSION OF FAITH REGARDING THE VISION GOD HAS GIVEN.

CONSIDER WHAT THE OUTCOME WOULD HAVE BEEN IF SOME OF THE STRONG LEADERS OF FAITH HAD DIFFERENT CONFESSIONS.

Joseph could have said, "I am my father's favorite son, and he has given me a coat of many colors. I will keep my mouth shut and my dreams to myself and enjoy this good life."

Moses could have said, "I am living the life of a Pharaoh's son here in Egypt. I will keep my mouth shut and stay right here and live this great life."

Joshua could have said, "I will stop right here at Jericho. We are in the Promised Land. We can enjoy what we have right here."

Nehemiah could have said, "I am in the Kings court as his cupbearer. This is a pretty good life. I will stay right here."

Esther could have said, "I will keep my mouth shut and continue to live as a queen. No one will ever have to know that I am a Jew who has been ordered to be slaughtered."

Daniel could have said, "I have favor with the King because I have interpreted his dream. I can keep my mouth shut and continue to live in the kings' court in his favor."

Peter and John could have said, "We preached, and 3,000 souls were saved in one day. We can stay here and pastor this church. We do not have to continue to put our lives on the line for the spread of the GOSPEL."

Each of these great heroes of faith could have stopped at a comfortable place, but each chose to fulfill their purpose in life to become a conduit of great blessing to others to the glory of God.

We must not stop in this comfortable place. We must press on toward the prize of the high calling of God in Christ Jesus to be a great blessing to the church and the world through the fulfillment of the vision that God has placed on each one of our hearts.

Be like Paul, who said, "I have fought a good fight. I have finished my course. I have kept the faith."

Finish your course. Prepare for your future through prayer by faith. SAY the vision that God has placed in your heart.

JUST BECAUSE IT IS WRITTEN DOES NOT MEAN THAT IT WILL AUTOMATICALLY

HAPPEN. YOU MUST PRAY IT THROUGH IN THE SPIRIT BEFORE IT WILL MANIFEST IN THE NATURAL. YOU MUST SPEAK IT INTO EXISTENCE. YOU MUST CONFESS IT WITH YOUR MOUTH AND BELIEVE IN YOUR HEART. YOU MUST MAKE PREPARATION. YOU MUST SAY IT.

When you accomplish the vision and God gives you victory over the antagonists, it will bring great glory to God, and your faith in God will grow exponentially.

2 Corinthians 4:17 (AMPC)
For our light, momentary affliction (this slight distress of the passing hour) is ever more and more abundantly preparing and producing and achieving for us an everlasting weight of glory [beyond all measure, excessively surpassing all comparisons and calculations, a vast and transcendent glory an blessedness never to cease!]

As you go through this time of sharing your vision, FOCUS ON YOUR HEART'S RELATIONSHIP TO GOD. BE FAITHFUL. WAIT ON GOD.

My prayer is that from this information, you have learned the importance of learning to think about everything that happens in life the way that God thinks about it, TRUSTING THAT HIS PLAN FOR YOU IS GOOD.

Jeremiah 29:11 (NKJV)
I know the plans that I have for you says the Lord, plans of good and not evil, to give you a future and a hope.

God wants you to know that "All things work together for good for those who love the Lord, who are the called according to His purpose (Romans 8:28)."

When you are faced with a trial, see it from God's perspective:
What mindset is HE changing?
What character trait is He making more like His?
What Kingdom principle is He establishing in our hearts and lives?
What battle is He preparing us to face and win?

2 Cor 10:4-5 (KJV)
Cast down imaginations and every high thing that exalts itself against the knowledge of God and bring into captivity every thought into the obedience of Christ.

Learn to say what God says about what He has called you to do!

Job 22:28 (NKJV)
You shall declare a thing and it shall be established for you!

SAY IT!!!

CHAPTER FOUR

WRITE IT

Habakkuk 2:2 (NKJV)
"Write the vision And make it plain on tablets, That he may run who reads it.

Writing something takes it from the realm of the invisible to the visible. Architects write out and draw out their plans. All laws are written. God wrote everything about each of us before we were born. God inspired men through the Holy Spirit to write the Bible so that we would know His will for us.

We must WRITE IT: Write the vision, that we might imprint it on our own minds, and make it clearer to ourselves, and especially that it might be made known and clear to others. What is handed down by word of mouth is easily misunderstood and open to corruption; what is written is clear and preserved.

A vision is a picture of how to solve a problem. When a vision is written or drawn out, the details of it become clearer. THE VISION IS NOT THE PLAN OR THE STRATEGY.

When I was a child and into young adulthood, I had a vision of becoming a doctor, one who brought healing to the sick and the wounded. I also had a vision of becoming a teacher. I did not understand how the two could be so similar. "Bringing inner healing to many students," is the "doctor" I became.

The writing of the vision does not mean that we know and understand how we will accomplish the vision. Often at this stage, most people have no idea how they will accomplish the vision. Most are sure that unless God does something miraculous, it cannot be done. This is a good thing. The vision that God gives is greater than we can accomplish under our own power. We all need God's power.

You were created to fulfill the vision that God placed in your heart.

Psalm 139:14,16 (AMP)
"(You) are fearfully and wonderfully made.... All the days ordained for (you) were written in (God's) book before one of them came to be."

Philippians 3:12 (TLB)
But I keep working toward that day when I will finally be all that Christ Jesus saved me for and wants me to be.

God gives each person a vision. Moses was 80 years old when he began to fulfill God's plan for his life. Colonel Sanders was 70 years old when he established Kentucky Fried Chicken. Caleb was 85 when he accomplished his vision and took possession of his piece of the Promised Land. One does not have to be young to accomplish a large vision.

One of the greatest hindrances of beginning a vision is fear. We may believe that if God really called a person to do a thing, that person would not be afraid. That is not true. God never removes the fear. Instead, He asks us to be strong and take courage. Courage is not the absence of fear but choosing to act in spite of the fear. Perfect love casts out fear.(1 John 4:18 NKJV)

When we love God and trust Him and love people enough to take a risk for their benefit, we can grow to a place where we are no longer afraid of that risk. But, we must first trust God to be our bravery and act on the things that He has given us to do. In time, the fear goes away.

God has promised to be your bravery.

Habakkuk 3:19 (AMPC)
The Lord God is my Strength, my personal bravery, and my invincible army; He makes my feet like hinds' feet and will make me to walk [not to stand still in terror, but to walk] and make [spiritual] progress upon my high places [of trouble, suffering, or responsibility]!

The first step in achieving the vision is to break through your fear, and trust God. You must begin to make steps toward the vision that God has placed in your heart.

Again, the vision is the picture of how to meet a need. Nehemiah asked what was going on in Jerusalem, and he listened.

NEHEMIAH 1:1-3 (NKJV)
The words of Nehemiah the son of Hachaliah.
It came to pass in the month of Chislev, in the twentieth year, as I was in Shushan the citadel, 2 that Hanani one of my brethren came with men from

Judah; and I asked them concerning the Jews who had escaped, who had survived the captivity, and concerning Jerusalem. ³ And they said to me, "The survivors who are left from the captivity in the province are there in great distress and reproach. The wall of Jerusalem is also broken down, and its gates are burned with fire."

We must allow this feeling to help others into our hearts. We cannot keep our hearts closed to other people. The idea of fulfilling the vision stays in your heart and mind. We are excited and empowered to complete the vision.

There is a burden for others deep in one's spirit from God. Write the things God gives about the situation. Research the problem more carefully. Ask God to confirm it. Meeting this need is something that He wants you to do. God will answer and confirm whether or not this concern is something He wants you to address. If it is, the burden for it will not go away until you complete what God has placed on your heart.

There is an understanding in your spirit that the vision is more than you can accomplish under your own power, yet there is a knowing in your spirit that meeting this need is something you must do. It takes great faith to do this. We must accept the responsibility to complete the vision.

It is necessary to spend time in fasting and prayer as we study the Word of God to receive the wisdom, understanding, strength, and power to complete the vision that God has placed in your heart, as Nehemiah did. We must ask God to reveal any underlying sins that created the problem. Underlying sin keeps God from unleashing HIS power. We must intercede on behalf of those who committed the sin that caused the judgment (See Nehemiah 1:4-6 and 8-11). The people who committed the sins were dead. Most needs that exist are because of sin. God disciplines people to get them to stop sinning. INTERCESSION can stop the judgment.

BECAUSE OF DAVID'S INTERCESSION, GOD STOPPED THE THREE YEAR FAMINE

II Samuel 21:1-3,6, 10, 14 (NKJV)
Now there was a famine in the days of David for three years, year after year; and David inquired of the Lord. And the Lord answered, "It is because of Saul and his bloodthirsty house, because he killed the Gibeonites." ²So the king called the Gibeonites and spoke to them. Now the Gibeonites were not of the children of Israel, but of the remnant of the Amorites; the children of Israel had sworn protection to them, but Saul had sought to kill them in his zeal for the children of Israel and Judah. Therefore David said to the Gibeonites,

"What shall I do for you? And with what shall I make atonement, that you may bless the inheritance of the Lord?" Let seven men of his descendants be delivered to us, and we will hang them before the Lord in Gibeah of Saul, whom the Lord chose"…from the beginning of harvest until the late rains poured on them from heaven…And after that God heeded the prayer for the land.

As God gives us a vision, He cleanses us, and He lifts us up to another level. When that portion of the vision is completed, He gives us a new vision or the vision grows, and He cleanses us in preparation for the next level.

God cleanses us at every level. Cleansing precedes the accomplishment of the vision. The cleaner the vessel, the more the power of God can come through you. The higher we go with God, the deeper the cleansing God will do, if we submit to him, and the greater the power that will flow through us in the form of discernment, wisdom, and power. We will be transformed as we are obedient and submitted to God to bring Him great glory.

God will bring you to a place where you have more assurance.

At this point, begin to claim the promises in the Bible for your Vision.

Nehemiah 1:9 (NKJV)
If you return to Me, and keep My commandments and do them, though some of you were cast out to the farthest part of the heavens, yet I will gather them from there, and bring them to the place which I have chosen as a dwelling for My name.'

God gives promises so we can ask Him to keep them.

WHAT IS THE PROMISE THAT GOD HAS MADE FOR THE FULFILLMENT OF YOUR VISION? You can ask God to show you the scriptures.

Matthew 6:33 (NKJV)
But seek first the kingdom of God and His righteousness, and all these things shall be added to you.

You become certain that God put the vision in your heart and that God will unleash His power to complete the vision.

This is a private transaction with you and God while you are in this period of intercession and confession of other people's sins and your own. God will let you know and affirm that He has indeed called you to complete the vision He has placed in your heart.

If you jump into a vision without processing through the vision with God and working with Him in prayer concerning the vision and your own issues, you may find yourself operating under your own power. But if God commissions you to do the vision, He will personally give you an assurance in your heart.

With that commission comes the confidence to pray for whatever you need to complete the vision.

Nehemiah 2:20 (NKJV)
The God of heaven himself will prosper us.

IN AN EFFORT TO PREPARE FOR MY VISION, I majored in Pre-medicine in college and even was accepted to medical school, but I just did not have a peace about it, so I did not go. I married Pierce while he was in the Air Force. When we were stationed in Maine, God called me to preach, teach, and heal. He gave me specific Scriptures from Isaiah 61:1-4 and Jeremiah 1:5.

For years, I struggled with my decision of not going to medical school. One day while Pierce was very ill in the hospital, God spoke to me and said that if I had become a doctor, I would have trusted in medicine to heal Pierce, rather than trusting Him. God miraculously healed Pierce, and God assured me that I made the right choice.

While we were living in Hendersonville, North Carolina, I was assisting Pierce in pastoring our first church, and God spoke to my heart to become a teacher. I had to go back to school to learn to become a teacher and get my certification to teach. At that time, I had no idea what God would do through me as a teacher. I only had the basic vision: become a teacher to teach others. This was a trying time for me. I was still struggling with uncertainty about whether I had missed God in not going to medical school. I started out as a substitute science teacher. A few weeks later, I was hired as a remedial math teacher in a middle school. As I prayed for my students, God gave me strategies and great favor to work with my students. All of my students increased more than two grade levels in one year. One student, who suffered from a traumatic brain injury in early childhood, increased six grade levels in one year. Again, God confirmed to me that I was to be a teacher. That June, we moved to Maryland, and our son was born in August. Weeks after he was born, friends from Maine came to me to tell me of a program at Bethesda Naval Hospital, where I could become a doctor. Again, I took this to God. I had a check in my spirit, and I did not feel comfortable leaving my children to do this.

A few months later, at the suggestion of a neighbor, I began the application process to the school system in Maryland. She said that it would take years for them to process my paperwork. I thought to myself, that would be fine. I wanted to wait until our baby was in school before I went back to work. Within days after submitting my paperwork, while in prayer at the foot of our bed, the Lord appeared to me in a vision and said, "I am going to place you in a school and I want you to witness for me every chance you get." I assumed this would be years later. A few days later, I received a call from the school system to come in to take their preliminary tests. Through a series of miracles, within a week, I was working part-time teaching science in a high school. This teaching position grew. I became the coordinator for a special program helping students who had potential but were performing poorly. God gave me wisdom and strategies to implement in this program. He also showed me demonic strongholds to tear down. It changed the students' lives, and it changed the school. These students went on to do great things with their lives.

One day after working in these programs for three years, God spoke to me and said I was doing exactly what He wanted me to do. I was opening blinded eyes and setting the captives free. From there, the vision changed and grew. God spoke to me about becoming the principal of a school, again opening blinded eyes and setting captives free and transforming an entire community. Each time there was a move up, there was a process of preparation and cleansing.

I shared this with you to help you to see how a vision can change and grow as God changes us and helps us to grow spiritually. God has great things for each of you to do.

WRITE IT!

CHAPTER 5

BELIEVE IT

We have been studying the process of reaching our Kingdom destiny.

It is encompassed in the saying: SEE IT, THINK IT, SAY IT, WRITE IT, BELIEVE IT, BE IT.

I am going to share a revelation God gave me to give an "understanding of God's ways" to encourage you in your Christian walk.

BELIEVE IT has everything to do with faith.
THE VALLEY Experience has everything to do with testing your faith.

Hebrews 11:1 (NKJV)
Now faith is the substance of things hoped for, the evidence of things not seen.

Acts 16:16-24 (NKJV)

[16] Now it happened, as we went to prayer, that a certain slave girl possessed with a spirit of divination met us, who brought her masters much profit by fortune-telling. [17] This girl followed Paul and us, and cried out, saying, "These men are the servants of the Most High God, who proclaim to us the way of salvation." [18] And this she did for many days.

But Paul, greatly annoyed, turned and said to the spirit, "I command you in the name of Jesus Christ to come out of her." And he came out that very hour. [19] But when her masters saw that their hope of profit was gone, they seized Paul and Silas and dragged them into the marketplace to the authorities.

[20] And they brought them to the magistrates, and said, "These men, being Jews, exceedingly trouble our city; [21] and they teach customs which are not lawful for us, being Romans, to receive or observe." [22] Then the multitude rose up together against them; and the magistrates tore off their clothes and commanded them to be beaten with rods. [23] And when they had laid many stripes on them, they threw them into prison, commanding the jailer to keep them securely. [24] Having received such a charge, he put them into the inner prison and fastened their feet in the stocks.

Paul and Silas were on their way to prayer. Paul, by the gift of discerning of spirits, recognized that this women who followed him for many days proclaiming that "these were men of the Most High God," was saying good things but by the wrong spirit: a spirit of divination. Paul cast this spirit of divination out of the woman.

With the spirit of divination gone, the woman could no longer tell fortunes, so her masters took Paul and Silas to the magistrates and lied about them, saying they were teaching things unlawful for Romans. Her masters incited the crowd to rise up against them. The magistrates had Paul and Silas beaten and thrown into prison without a trial, all because they delivered a young girl from a demonic spirit of divination on their way to a prayer meeting. How many of us could respond as Paul did in such a situation?

There is a purpose for our trials and Valley Experiences.

JESUS UNDERSTANDS OUR PAIN BECAUSE HE HAS BEEN THERE. HE SUFFERED MANY PAINS AND WAS FALSELY ACCUSED. BUT HE ROSE IN VICTORY!

JESUS' TESTING IN THE WILDERNESS

Matthew 4:1-11 (NKJV)

Then Jesus was led up by the Spirit into the wilderness to be tempted by the devil. ² And when He had fasted forty days and forty nights, afterward He was hungry. ³ Now when the tempter came to Him, he said, "If You are the Son of God, command that these stones become bread."

⁴ But He answered and said, "It is written, 'Man shall not live by bread alone, but by every word that proceeds from the mouth of God.'"

⁵ Then the devil took Him up into the holy city, set Him on the pinnacle of the temple, 6 and said to Him, "If You are the Son of God, throw Yourself down. For it is written:
'He shall give His angels charge over you,' and, 'In their hands they shall bear you up, Lest you dash your foot against a stone.'"

⁷ Jesus said to him, "It is written again, 'You shall not tempt the Lord your God.'"

⁸ Again, the devil took Him up on an exceedingly high mountain, and showed Him all the kingdoms of the world and their glory. ⁹ And he said to Him, "All these things I will give You if You will fall down and worship me."

¹⁰ Then Jesus said to him, "Away with you, Satan! For it is written, 'You shall worship the Lord your God, and Him only you shall serve.'"

¹¹ Then the devil left Him, and behold, angels came and ministered to Him.

The Holy Spirit empowered Jesus for ministry to withstand the scoffers and unbelievers, to withstand burden of carrying all of our sins to the death on the cross, to do the work done in the underworld and secure the keys of death, hell, and the grave, triumphing over Satan, the enemy, to preach to many who had died previously, to ascend in victory back to His Father in heaven, to be seated at God's right hand, and to eternally make intercession for the saints.

Immediately after receiving this wonderful, powerful, promotion, Jesus was led into the wilderness- A VALLEY EXPERIENCE to be tested. Wilderness or valley experiences are dry and uncomfortable, painful, and never pleasant. Dry, meaning spiritually dry means not hearing from God for an extended period of time.

THE TEST WAS: "Will you do what I told you to do when your flesh, soul (mind, will and emotions) and spirit are tested intensely to test your limitations near to the point of death?"

Now that I have given you this great power, without measure, what will you do when you are tempted and tested in intensity?

God will test us before He places us in leadership. We must be proven before we can lead.

Jesus' first test was of the flesh, the BODY. He was exceedingly hungry, having fasted for forty days. Jesus could have used His unlimited power to turn stones into bread. Jesus would not end this test of the flesh even though He had the power to end this painful, miserable test. He stayed in the struggle in obedience to the change that God was making in Him. Jesus answered the test with the Word of God. Even though Jesus responded appropriately, He still was not yet released to eat. The intense testing of Jesus' flesh was necessary to prepare Him for the horrible beating, crucifixion, and death on the cross He had to endure.

One's soul is made of the mind, will, and emotions. The next test was of Jesus' relationship to the Father and the emotional and psychological ties wrapped up in that. His SOUL was tested. The test was to prove his relationship with His Father, prove His identity, prove His call, and prove that God always has His back. It was similar to the test of Shadrach, Meshach, and Abednego when they would not bow down to another god. They stated that "their God was able to deliver them, but, even if He did not, He was able to." Again, Jesus answered appropriately with the word: "thou shall not tempt the Lord they God." Jesus had no need to prove who He was or to exhibit His great power. Even though Jesus responded appropriately, He still was not yet released to eat.

The last test was of the spirit of man. His SPIRIT was tested. Pride is a sin of the spirit of man. Satan said that he would give Jesus all of the kingdoms of the earth if He would bow down to him. To reconcile and take back all of the kingdoms of the earth was a big part of the call and purpose of Jesus coming to earth in human form. This would have been an easy way to fulfill a big part of His call through a momentary switch of allegiance. Part of Jesus' purpose could have been easily and quickly completed without pain, without suffering, without rejection, and without the most painful and shameful death on the cross.

But all must be done God's way and in God's plan. Again, Jesus answered with the word and with obedience: "Thou shalt worship the Lord our God, and Him alone shall you serve."

In Jesus' example, we see that in the valley experiences, we are tested in our total being- our body, soul, and spirit. We are to answer with the Word of God to every test. We are to remain faithful to God and trust in Him and not give up. God builds His Character in us, increases our faith, and shapes us into His image in the trials and brings blessings and salvation to others.

1 Peter 1:6-7 (NKJV)
In this you greatly rejoice, though now for a little while, if need be, you have been grieved by various trials, that the genuineness of your faith, being much more precious than gold that perishes, though it is tested by fire, may be found to praise, honor, and glory at the revelation of Jesus Christ.

Like silver, gold is purified in the fire. Impurities are burned away.

James 1:1-8,12 (NIV)
Consider it pure joy, my brothers and sisters, whenever you face trials of many kinds, because you know that the testing of your faith produces perseverance. Let perseverance finish its work so that you may be mature and complete, not lacking anything. If any of you lacks wisdom, you should ask God, who gives generously to all without finding fault, and it will be given to you. ...

Blessed is the one who perseveres under trial because, having stood the test, that person will receive the crown of life that the Lord has promised to those who love him.

We are "transformed" in the fire of testing. It is painful and not pleasant."

Our faith grows in the trial. We learn to persevere and become stable in our faith. We learn God's ways and grow closer to Him.

1 Peter 4:12 (NKJV)
Beloved, think it not strange, the fiery trial which is to try you as though some strange thing has happened unto you: But rejoice, inasmuch as ye are partakers of Christ's sufferings; that when his glory shall be revealed, ye may glad also with exceeding joy.

Habakkuk 3:17-19 (AMP)
Though the fig tree does not blossom, there is no fruit on the vine, the product of the olive fails, and the fields yield no food, the flock is cut off from the fold, and there are no cattle in the stall. Yet, I will rejoice in the Lord. I will exult the victorious God of my salvation. The Lord God is my Strength, my personal bravery and my invincible army. He makes my feet like hinds feet and will make me to walk, not stand still in terror, but to walk and make spiritual progress on my high places of struggle, suffering, or responsibility!"

These Scriptures from Habakkuk is now part of my testimony. It makes it very clear that when we respond as we should in the testing, we grow spiritually.

I did not know how to fight the enemy of my soul, but God taught me how to skillfully use His Word, like an arrow shot from a bow of bronze, to destroy the enemy while he is still far away.

2 Cor. 10:3-5
For though we walk in the flesh, we do not war after the flesh:
⁴ (For the weapons of our warfare are not carnal, but mighty through God to the pulling down of strong holds;) ⁵ Casting down imaginations, and every high thing that exalteth itself against the knowledge of God, and bringing into captivity every thought to the obedience of Christ;

Learning to fight using spiritual weapons is what brings us great victory. In the trials, we learn to fight God's way and bring God great glory!

As we learn to fight using spiritual weapons, we praise God in everything. We seek God for His wisdom. We learn to use His Word in prayer and in declaration to fight the enemy that is unseen.

A leadership development specialist said, "The single best way to develop leaders is to take people out of their safe environment and away from people they know, and throw them into a new arena they know little about. Way over their head. In fact, the more demanding the challenges, and more pressure and risk they face, the more likely a dynamic leader will emerge."

This sounds unsafe and unkind, but it is how God develops leaders, with one difference. God is right there, controlling the intensity and duration like a goldsmith purifying gold. He provides just enough heat to purify, but not to destroy.

You will experience a valley or wasteland experience. You will get to a place where you feel like you are wandering in an endless desert, and God has abandoned you.

This is how Joshua and Caleb felt wandering through the desert with Israel when they had done nothing wrong to deserve it. This is how Joseph felt when he served time in prison for a crime he did not commit. He had done nothing wrong, and he felt like God had abandoned him and his dream. This is how David felt wandering from cave to cave, hiding in fear of his life when he was anointed to be king. This is how Gideon felt when he considered himself the least of the least. This is how Daniel felt when he was thrown into the lion's den. This is how Paul and Silas were tempted to feel when they were thrown into prison when they had done nothing wrong. You may feel adrift in anger and confusion. Imagine how Jesus felt as he was betrayed by one of his own, abandoned by those closest to him, falsely accused when he had done only good and nothing wrong, beaten beyond recognition and crucified.

He went through this to set us free from sin, and so that He could be touched by our infirmities (understands our weakness, empathize with our pain, and knows how to pray for us) because He lives to make intercession for us.

The valley or wasteland experience is an important process. The valley is the place where God transforms you into the person who can fulfill the vision that God placed in your heart. God matures you.

When God seems absent and everything is going wrong, will you trust God enough to prepare you for what is ahead?

A dream or a vision costs you something. Count the cost.
- Are you willing to pay the price to be able to complete your vision?
- Do you believe in God enough to trust His purpose and accept His plan for preparation, even if you don't understand or agree with it?

Trials are very valuable experiences that have eternal implications.

ACTS 16:25-40 (NKJV)
[25] But at midnight Paul and Silas were praying and singing hymns to God, and the prisoners were listening to them. [26] Suddenly there was a great earthquake, so that the foundations of the prison were shaken; and immediately all the doors were opened and everyone's chains were loosed. [27] And the keeper of the prison, awaking from sleep and seeing the prison doors open, supposing the prisoners had fled, drew his sword and was about to kill himself. [28] But Paul called with a loud voice, saying, "Do yourself no harm, for we are all here."
[29] Then he called for a light, ran in, and fell down trembling before Paul and Silas. [30] And he brought them out and said, "Sirs, what must I do to be saved?" [31] So they said, "Believe on the Lord Jesus Christ, and you will be saved, you and your household." [32] Then they spoke the word of the Lord to him and to all who were in his house. [33] And he took them the same hour of the night and washed their stripes. And immediately he and all his family were baptized. [34] Now when he had brought them into his house, he set food before them; and he rejoiced, having believed in God with all his household.
[35] And when it was day, the magistrates sent the officers, saying, "Let those men go."

[36] So the keeper of the prison reported these words to Paul, saying, "The magistrates have sent to let you go. Now therefore depart, and go in peace."
[37] But Paul said to them, "They have beaten us openly, uncondemned Romans, and have thrown us into prison. And now do they put us out secretly? No indeed! Let them come themselves and get us out."
[38] And the officers told these words to the magistrates, and they were afraid when they heard that they were Romans. [39] Then they came and pleaded with them and brought them out, and asked them to depart from the city. [40] So they went out of the prison and entered the house of Lydia; and when they had seen the brethren, they encouraged them and departed.

God gives us interesting insights into His WAYS as we study Scripture. In this account of Paul, one can see how God received the glory in this trying situation.

Paul and Silas began to pray and sing hymns and praise God in the night while chained in their prison cell. As we praise God, it releases His power into our situation. The other prisoners heard Paul and Silas praying and singing and praising God. It was at that moment that God showed up! God sent an earthquake into the prison. The prison gates flew open, and their chains fell off.

This natural description has a spiritual implication. When we learn to praise God in every situation, the lies that the enemy has told to hold us in bondage are immediately exposed and have no power to hold us any longer.

Upon observing this, the jailer thought that all his prisoners had escaped and planned to kill himself before his boss did.

Paul cried out to the jailer, letting him know that they were all still in jail. This action by Paul was a word of wisdom. The jailer was astounded that all of the prisoners stayed in their cells when they could have escaped. He cried out, "Sirs, what must I do to be saved?" Paul, by a word of wisdom, was made aware of what God was doing in this event and chose to stay to minister to the jailer and his family. It is so important to hear what God is saying to us in every situation, but especially in the trials because it is in our obedience in the trials, that God gets the greatest glory!

God used Paul and Silas at this moment to bring salvation to the jailer, his whole household, and for all in the jail to witness the power of God!

How many of us are willing to be subjected to mistreatment so that others can be saved?

Not only were the jailer and his whole household saved, but Paul and Silas were also vindicated and freed! The magistrates personally came and publicly apologized and set them free. GOD WAS GLORIFIED!!!

Know that there is a divine purpose for the pain.
Birthing comes through sorrow.
Every good fruit you produce comes through suffering.

God has planted his seed in us through the Holy Spirit. When you see the sorrow multiply, it is a sign that God is getting ready to send something to you.

For every struggle in your life, God desires to accomplish something in your character and your spirit. He wishes to produce much fruit. When the pain is at its ultimate expression, it is time to push. WE PUSH BY PRAYER AND PRAISE.

There is an acronym for push:
PRAY
UNTIL
SOMETHING
HAPPENS

We must keep on pushing until the baby is birthed. We push the baby out by praising God in the trial. We must praise Him when things seem to be their worst. God will cause us to deliver the fruit.

John 16:20-21
Verily, verily, I say unto you, That ye shall weep and lament, but the world shall rejoice: and ye shall be sorrowful, but your sorrow shall be turned into joy.
[21] A woman when she is in travail hath sorrow, because her hour is come: but as soon as she is delivered of the child, she remembereth no more the anguish, for joy that a man is born into the world.

John 15:16 (NKJV)
You did not choose Me, but I chose you and appointed you that you should go and bear fruit, and that your fruit should remain, that whatever you ask the Father in My name He may give you.

AS WE FACE TRIALS IN THIS LIFE, KNOW IT IS NOT IN VAIN. GOD DESIRES TO USE YOU TO BRING GLORY TO HIS NAME AND TO BLESS YOU BEYOND WHAT YOU CAN IMAGINE.

There is a purpose for our pain. Believe what God says, no matter what you go through. It is in our weakness that God shows up the greatest!

2 Corinthians 4:7-10 (NKJV)
But we have this treasure in earthen vessels, that the excellence of the power may be of God and not of us. ⁸ We are hard-pressed on every side, yet not crushed; we are perplexed, but not in despair; ⁹ persecuted, but not forsaken; struck down, but not destroyed— ¹⁰ always carrying about in the body the dying of the Lord Jesus, that the life of Jesus also may be manifested in our body

2 Cor. 4:17 (AMP)
For our light, momentary affliction (this slight distress of the passing hour) is ever more and more abundantly preparing and producing and achieving for us an everlasting weight of glory [beyond all measure, excessively surpassing all comparisons and all calculations, a vast and transcendent glory and blessedness never to cease!

BELIEVE IT!

CHAPTER 6

BE IT

The purpose of the conclusion of this book is to help people to understand the steps necessary to fulfill their destinies. The process is capsulized in the statements:

SEE IT, THINK IT, SAY IT, WRITE IT, BELIEVE IT, BE IT

You have a special identity and destiny that is uniquely your own.

God has a plan for your life. He says in Jeremiah 29:11 (ESV), "I know the plans I have for you…" And in Psalm 139:16 (NKJV), "In Your book they all were written, The days fashioned for me, When as yet there were none of them."

See yourself there.

Philippians 3:12-14 (NKJV)
[12] Not that I have already attained,[a] or am already perfected; but I press on, that I may lay hold of that for which Christ Jesus has also laid hold of me. [13] Brethren, I do not count myself to have [b]apprehended; but one thing I do, forgetting those things which are behind and reaching forward to those things which are ahead, [14] I press toward the goal for the prize of the upward call of God in Christ Jesus.

There is a purposed place for you. Take the Seven Nations.

Deuteronomy 7:1-2 (NKJV)
"When the Lord your God brings you into the land which you go to possess, and has cast out many nations before you, the Hittites and the Girgashites and the Amorites and the Canaanites and the Perizzites and the Hivites and the Jebusites, seven nations greater and mightier than you.

Each one of these seven nations that Joshua and the people of Israel conquered in the Promised Land represents some aspect of our current society. Are you in your designated place? The nation or nations to which you have been assigned are the realms of our society where God will use you to impact and transform and take dominion in the spirit.

Joshua 21:43-45 (NKJV)
[43] So the Lord gave to Israel all the land of which He had sworn to give to their fathers, and they took possession of it and dwelt in it. [44] The Lord gave them rest all around, according to all that He had sworn to their fathers. And not a man of all their enemies stood against them; the Lord delivered all their enemies into their hand. [45] Not a word failed of any good thing which the Lord had spoken to the house of Israel. All came to pass.

This conquering and destroying are of demonic spiritual strongholds that inhabit that realm, not people. This demonic confederacy is seven spirits in the seven nations.

There is a place you are supposed to take. For me, that place was and is the educational system and the religious system. For David, his place was from Hebron to Jebus. (JERUSALEM)

God has a way of transferring ownership of titles. David was concerned that the tribe of Benjamin had never fully driven the Jebusites out of the Promised Land. David, who was from the tribe of JUDAH, was determined to do it, to take possession of all that God promised.

Likewise, God wants us to be determined to possess all that He has promised to us.

2 Samuel 5:6-7,9-12 (NLT)
⁶ David then led his men to Jerusalem to fight against the Jebusites, the original inhabitants of the land who were living there. The Jebusites taunted David, saying, "You'll never get in here! Even the blind and lame could keep you out!" For the Jebusites thought they were safe. ⁷ But David captured the fortress of Zion, which is now called the City of David.
⁹ So David made the fortress his home, and he called it the City of David. He extended the city, starting at the supporting terraces and working inward. ¹⁰ And David became more and more powerful, because the Lord God of Heaven's Armies was with him.¹¹ Then King Hiram of Tyre sent messengers to David, along with cedar timber and carpenters and stonemasons, and they built David a palace. ¹² And David realized that the Lord had confirmed him as king over Israel and had blessed his kingdom for the sake of his people Israel.

Write down your vision!

(Habakkuk 2:2)

Write the vision and make it plain

The place was occupied by an enemy shouting threats. You will silence the voice of the adversary by your own declarations of the Word of God.

Go into the place God has told you. David took the stronghold of Zion by faith.

Will you take back the stronghold of the place God has given you?

Matthew 11:12 (NKJV)
The kingdom of heaven suffers violence and the violent take it by force.

You have to be extreme about it!

David called Jebus, the City of David. He called the city by his name.
Call the place God has given you by your name. You must make it your own.

While others may help you, you must lead. Only you can lead this ministry as God has spoken it to you. Only you have the direct revelation from God on this ministry. Only you have the anointing from God to carry it through. If you give it to someone else to do, they will shipwreck it. If you give it to someone else, it will never be what God placed in your heart.

I know two people who did that. It was heartbreaking to see what became of the ministries they gave away and let others lead. They had a beautiful vision and plan, but they gave it away for someone else to do while they assisted. Each was a shipwreck. No one else will do it like the vision God gave you concerning it. Make the ministry your own. Take possession of it. You must do it.

-If you are going to take what God has for you, you must occupy it
 (military occupation) before you can possess it.

-Go and spy out the land and make declarations over it before you can possess it.

-Believe you will receive it, and you shall have it. Declare it by faith!

The blind (meaning those who do not have the vision) and the lame (meaning those who do not have the strength of God to do the vision) cannot stop you. Possess the city. Know that God has made you a king and a royal priesthood.

The City of David is the Jerusalem we know today. Jerusalem is God's chosen city. This city has great spiritual significance. In Scripture, Jerusalem is symbolic of the church.

As David took the city from the enemy, we are to take the place that God has given unto us for God's glory! Do you know that we are the temple of God? The Holy Spirit dwells in us, in you and in me! We are the house of God. It is our very identity. God wants us to be a place where He will dwell, where angels will ascend and descend on assignment, and where the heavens are open over a people who abide in Him. We must set our hearts on being a House filled with His glory wherever we go. Our goal is to agree with heaven at all times. As we agree with God's Word, the gates of heaven are open, where angels are released on assignment from God.

Matthew 16:19 (NASB)
Whatever we bind on earth shall have been bound in heaven, and whatever we loose on earth shall have been loosed in heaven.

When you are in your place, God will use you to speak heavenly things into existence on earth and to bind those things that are not according to His will. We are to bring healing, deliverance, and blessing everywhere we go.

Shortly, before I became a teacher at a High School in Maryland, God spoke to me about what He wanted me to do there. He told me to "Restore sight to the blind and to set the captives free." This came through a program that was created and designed as God gave me insights and strategies to put it into place, in working with students. Seven years prior, God called me to minister from Isaiah 61:1-4 (AMPC), which is rephrased, in part, in Luke 4:18-19(AMPC) by Jesus. These Scriptures contain the essence of the direction to restore sight to the blind and to set the captives free.

I did not understand what this meant, initially, in the context of the educational system, but three years into the process, God gave me revelation. Revelation opens up new realms of living, of possibility, and of faith. It is necessary to receive regular revelation from God. It is important to pray declarations for revelation regularly. Scripture tells us, "My people are destroyed for a lack of knowledge (Hosea 4:6)." A more complete translation is, "Without a prophetic revelation, the people go unrestrained, walking in circles, having no destiny."

God spoke to me and said, "Before you started this program, these students did not see who they were in Me. They had no vision for their lives. They were blind. As a result of their blindness, they were held in captivity by the enemy from becoming all that they were meant to be."

But now, their sight has been restored, and they have been set free.

As you are in the process of fulfilling your destiny, take possession of your call, "BE IT," and become the person God destined you to be. There will be trials or tests that one will have to face in fulfilling the vision God has given you.

There are four major stages to bring your vision to fruition. These stages or evaluations will mature your relationship with God. You will learn to know God at another level. It makes one spiritually stronger, with a more Godly Character.

1. Obtaining the Resources and Finances to Fulfill the Vision

Nehemiah 2:7-8 (AMPC)
Also I said to the king, If it pleases the king, let letters be given me for the governors beyond the [Euphrates] River, that they may let me pass through to Judah,8 And a letter to Asaph, keeper of the king's forest or park, that he may give me timber to make beams for the gates of the fortress of the temple and

for the city wall and for the house that I shall occupy. And the king granted what I asked, for the good hand of my God was upon me.

The Biblical model for obtaining resources is to raise the money by asking people to help. Those who take the responsibility will go ask others to help and will raise the money to complete what God has placed on their hearts.

In my situation, we prepared a description of our program and the things that would be needed to establish and maintain the program. We wrote a proposal. We met and talked with the principal about the resources, staff and finances that would be needed to complete this task. In addition, we personally met with over 50 different businesses in the community to solicit their support: through finances, mentors, job shadowing sites, and more. The principal gave limited finances and assigned four staff persons to assist in teaching, giving one class period a day for the year for each. The rest came from the businesses that agreed to support our program.

2. Re-Evaluation and Restructuring Personal Responsibilities

If God adds a new vision, then something will need to come off our plates. The more significant of a leader you are, the more difficult. In Nehemiah 2:5-6, Nehemiah asked to be sent to Judah for a set time to rebuild the city.

Nehemiah 2:5-6 (NKJV)
5 And I said to the king, "If it pleases the king, and if your servant has found favor in your sight, I ask that you send me to Judah, to the city of my fathers' tombs, that I may rebuild it."
6 Then the king said to me (the queen also sitting beside him), "How long will your journey be? And when will you return?" So it pleased the king to send me; and I set him a time.

We must learn to walk in freedom in the Word of God. When we tear down strongholds and change mindsets, God breaks a curse. We must renew our minds as the baby weaned from nursing or a bottle. Not only do we have to learn to think differently, but we must learn to walk in that new level. We must let go of some things to have time and strength to do the new thing that God has placed on our hearts. We must renew our minds on the Word of God and be led by the Spirit of God as He teaches us to know and understand how to function in new levels.

3. Seeing the Whole Magnitude of the Issue

For the programs that I ran, an investigation of the academic, emotional, and home situations of the students entering the program was done. This was important in understanding those things that impacted their thinking and development. An investigation of the level of instruction the students had received and would be receiving, and their past performance was completed. In addition, God revealed the mindsets of the teachers and staff that would be teaching these students and how to change wrong mindsets in teachers, staff, and students. God revealed what was needed to bridge the gaps and deficiencies in learning and restore the vision of the students. God revealed what was needed: to provide the instruction, educational and emotional supports, and encouragement that were needed to restore, bring healing, and advance these students.

4. Engaging Those That Will Support the Vision

Nehemiah 2:17-18 (AMPC)
Then I said to them, You see the bad situation we are in—how Jerusalem lies in ruins, and its gates are burned with fire. Come, let us build up the wall of Jerusalem, that we may no longer be a disgrace.
[18] Then I told them of the hand of my God which was upon me for good, and also the words that the king had spoken to me. And they said, Let us rise up and

build! So they strengthened their hands for the good work.

    a.   Describe the need. Get others emotionally involved in the vision.
    b.   Give a testimony of what God did and what the leader did to support the vision.
    c.   Share miracles that have happened. Call for a verbal commitment.
    d.   Enable people to start work right away.

There were meetings with principals, school system officials, leaders of businesses, students, staff, parents, and many others to recruit and enlist the finances, resources, and specialized staff necessary to run and maintain this program. God touched peoples' hearts to support and participate in many ways.

5. Walking Through the Experience of Rejection.

People will laugh at you, despise you, question you, criticize you, and misread your motives. You cannot defend yourself because it goes with the territory. The hurt is repetitive. Unforgiveness can set in, causing one to isolate, become hard, and die inside.

Pressure came from colleagues, administrators, parents, students, staff members, and people from the community that did all of the above. God strengthened us and carried us through all of it, victoriously.

Rejection can cause suffering, which requires tremendous humility to walk through. Do good to those who hurt you. Do not retain bitterness and unforgiveness. Ask God to give you strength and grace to become like Christ.

6. The Process of Dealing with Untruths.

This happens early in the launch of the vision from an important person. A rumor will come from another person to you. Usually, they are envious. It can cause you to doubt your vision. Hear it, think about it, and move on.

There were rumors from teachers and counselors who said this program would never work, and they lied about results to undermine it. They would talk about me and give our students a hard time. Yet, during school performance evaluations, they would want to use our data of success with these students to make the report for the overall school performance look good. COMPLETE THE VISION- IT SILENCES THE RUMORS.

7. The Process of Coming to Completion

I finished the assignment given to me. These students went on to do great things. Seventy percent went on to do well in honors-level classes in high school. These same students went on to college, military or trade school and finished well. Hundreds and hundreds of students were transformed to become successful examples of God's power and grace with a vision and a destiny that is transforming the lives of many others.

Finding and fulfilling one's destiny is so important. While we may be tremendously blessed to see what God will do through us as we obey, it is not just about us! It is about God and those whom He wants to bless through us. We are His children and a big part of His Kingdom plan. God is looking for His church to do as He declared in the beginning, "To be fruitful, multiply and have dominion in the earth" until the kingdoms of this world become the kingdoms of our God! This is our assignment! This is our destiny! This is our call!

SEE IT, THINK IT, SAY IT, WRITE IT, BELIEVE IT, BE IT!

Revelation 11:15 (NKJV)
Then the seventh angel sounded: And there were loud voices in heaven, saying, "The kingdoms of this

world have become the kingdoms of our Lord and of His Christ, and He shall reign forever and ever!"

ABOUT THE AUTHOR

Thelma C. Smith served in the public education system for over twenty-three years as a secondary school principal, assistant principal, and science teacher, helping students to fulfill their destinies and maximize their potential.

She has served for the past forty years in various ministries as a Co-pastor, Assistant Pastor, Bible School Coordinator, Adult and Children's Sunday School Coordinator and Teacher, and a Women's Ministry Leader.

In 2010, she published a book entitled, A Bride Without Spot or Wrinkle. The purpose of that book was to focus prayer in spiritual realms to bring deliverance to woman, and restoration and transformation to the body of Christ.

Rev. Smith resides in Virginia with her husband, Rev. Pierce Smith. They are the proud parents of 3 wonderful children and six beautiful grandchildren.

REFERENCE

1. "H3529 - Kĕbar - Strong's Hebrew Lexicon (KJV)." Blue Letter Bible. Accessed 1 Oct, 2019. https://www.blueletterbible.org//lang/lexicon/lexicon.cfm?Strongs=h3529&t=kjv

INDEX

A

abundance, 18, 20, 49, 51, 58
accusations, 11
addiction, 9–10
adultery, 7–9
alcohol, 9–10
angels, 3, 81, 102, 110
anointing, 5, 44–45, 100
assignment, 5, 102, 110

B

battle, 38, 60, 64
beliefs, 46
bitterness, 5, 109
blessings, 4, 21, 30, 37–38, 84, 102
bondage, 9, 14, 35, 41, 44, 59, 92
bravery, 69
businesses, 54, 59, 105, 108

C

captives, 4, 9, 14, 25–27, 29, 43, 46, 76–77, 103
cave, 31, 56, 88
Christ Jesus, 41–42, 53, 62, 68, 97
church, 3, 7–8, 13, 22, 57, 60, 62, 75, 102, 110
circumcision, 35
commandments, 17, 39, 73
confession, 61, 73
corruption, 54, 67
courage, 19, 68
courageous, 50–51
curse, 29, 34, 36–38, 106

D

death, 5, 13–14, 82–84
debt, 31
declarations, 24, 87, 100–101
deliverance, 4, 12, 34–35, 60, 102, 112
depression, 10, 39
despair, 31, 95
devil, 81
disgrace, 30, 107
distress, 31, 63, 95
divination, 79–80
dominion, 18, 26–27, 38, 98, 110
dreams, 19, 23, 59, 61, 88–89
drugs, 9–10

E

earthquake, 91
embarrassment, 8
emotions, 6, 9, 26, 82–83
enemy, 11–12, 24, 27, 34, 42, 45–46, 55, 82, 87, 92, 98, 102, 104
escape, 9–10
excellence, 45, 95

F

famine, 34, 59, 71
fear, 2, 12, 20, 29–31, 34, 37–39, 41–44, 55, 68–69, 88
forgiveness, 11, 19, 34, 46
fortress, 99, 104
fulfillment, 62, 73

G

gates, 70, 102, 104, 107
generations, 34, 36
glory, 4, 16, 24–27, 32, 62–63, 81, 85–86, 91, 94–95, 102
gold, 22, 32, 85
grain, 6, 45, 59
guard, 41–43, 49, 53–54
guilt, 11

H

harvest, 6, 72
healing, 4, 6, 13, 29, 67, 102, 107
heartbreaking, 101
heaven, 72–74, 82, 100, 102, 110
Holy Spirit, 13, 27, 45, 53, 66, 82, 93, 102
hopeless, 14–15

I

impartation, 13
inabilities, 29
instructions, 5, 7, 51, 107
intercession, 71, 73, 82, 89

J

joy, 24, 39, 85–86, 94
judgment, 14, 71

K

kingdom principle, 58, 64
kingdoms, 73, 81, 84, 99–100, 110–11
knowledge, 43–45, 64, 87, 103

L

lamentation, 4

leaders, 13–14, 87–88, 106, 108
life, 8–10, 13–14, 16, 18, 35, 40, 44, 46, 49, 58, 61–63, 68, 85, 88, 93–96
Lord, 2, 5, 12, 14–15, 17, 19–21, 25–26, 39–40, 50, 52, 64, 71–72, 81, 83–86, 97–99
love, 10, 12, 30, 39, 58, 64, 85

M

magistrates, 79–80, 90–91, 93
mentors, 23, 105
minister, 8, 92, 103
ministry, 8, 13–14, 22, 60, 82, 100–101, 112
miracles, 12–13, 76, 108
momentary affliction, 63, 95
money, 105
Moses, 59, 61, 68
mouth, 12, 40, 49–52, 57, 61–63, 67

N

nations, 14, 26, 31, 97–98

O

obedience, 21, 26, 43, 57, 64, 83–84, 87, 92
officers, 90–91

P

pain, 4–5, 9–10, 80, 84, 89, 93–94
paperwork, 76
Passover, 34–35, 38
peace, 10, 13, 41–43, 53, 74, 91
persecution, 56
perseverance, 85
picture, 67, 69
possession, 2, 36–37, 51, 68, 98–99, 101, 104
poverty, 37
power, 20, 22, 24, 27, 36, 38–39, 43–44, 46, 67, 70–74, 83–84, 91–92, 95, 110
power of God, 2, 19, 72, 92
praise, 3, 6, 35, 85, 93–94
praiseworthy, 43, 54
pray, 12, 43, 53, 59–60, 63, 74, 89, 91, 93
prayer, 9, 24, 41, 48, 53, 59, 62–63, 71–72, 74, 76, 79, 87, 93
praying, 44, 90
pressure, 88, 108
principalities, 36
prison, 79–80, 88, 90–91
prodigal, 8
prodigal son, 7–9
program, 22–24, 54, 58–59, 75–76, 103, 105, 107–9
Promised Land, 2, 30–31, 34, 36–37, 51, 55, 60–61, 68, 97–98
promotion, 3–6, 15, 29–30, 82

prophecy, 11, 15
prophesy, 4, 14

R

recognition, 89
rejection, 84, 108–9
resources, 8, 20, 104–5, 108
restoration, 4, 6, 60, 112
resurrection, 13
revelation, 7, 42, 85, 103, 110
risk, 68–69, 88

S

sacrifice, 21, 25
salvation, 20, 39, 50, 79, 84, 86, 92
Satan, 81–82, 84
school, 22–23, 56, 75–77
scriptures, 18, 45, 51, 73–74, 86, 91, 102–3
servants, 79, 106
set, 11, 26, 28, 33, 35–36, 47, 59, 81, 89, 93, 102–4, 106, 108
shame, 29, 31
silence, 100, 109
situation, 11, 14–15, 32–33, 57, 70, 80, 91–92, 105
sorrow, 21, 93–94
souls, 6, 10, 60, 62, 82–84, 87

strength, 3, 22, 26–27, 39, 69, 71, 86, 101, 106, 109
strongholds, 100, 106
students, 22–24, 58–59, 67, 75–76, 103, 107–10
supervisor, 29, 32
supplication, 41, 53

T

teachers, 9, 29, 46, 58, 67, 75, 103, 107, 109, 112
temple, 4, 81, 102, 104
tempt, 24, 81, 83
testimony, 86, 108
thanksgiving, 41, 53
transformation, 28, 31–32, 34, 112
treasury, 49
tribe, 2, 6, 8, 35, 98
trust, 68, 84, 89
trusting, 38, 64, 75
truth, 11, 20, 41, 45–46

U

unbelievers, 82
understanding, 7, 27, 41–44, 53, 57–58, 70–71, 107
unforgiveness, 108–9
unworthy, 30–31

V

valley, 4, 14, 80, 82, 84, 88–89
victory, 19, 36, 63, 80, 82
virtue, 43, 45, 54
vision, 16, 18, 21, 23, 25–26, 51, 56, 58–60, 62–63, 66–74, 76–77, 89, 99–101, 103–5, 107–10
voices, 90, 100, 110

W

watchman, 2, 7–9, 11
wealth, 20, 37–38, 59–60
weapons, 87
wilderness, 55, 80–82
wisdom, 3, 20, 24, 30, 40, 43–44, 57–58, 71–72, 76, 85, 87, 92
witness, 3, 24–25, 76, 92
worship, 33, 81

www.ingramcontent.com/pod-product-compliance
Lightning Source LLC
Chambersburg PA
CBHW052150110526
44591CB00012B/1924